The Lady of
SUDELEY

The Lady of
SUDELEY

JEAN BRAY

SUTTON PUBLISHING

This book was first published in 2000 by
Long Barn Books

This edition first published in 2004 by
Sutton Publishing Limited · Phoenix Mill
Thrupp · Stroud · Gloucestershire · GL5 2BU

British Library Cataloguing in Publication Data
A catalogue record for this book is available from the
British Library.

ISBN 0 7509 3720 3

Typeset in 12/14pt Photina.
Typesetting and origination by
Sutton Publishing Limited.
Printed and bound in Great Britain by
J.H. Haynes & Co. Ltd, Sparkford.

Jean Bray has been a writer and journalist for more than forty years, starting her career in Africa. She came to London to work on *The Daily Herald* and has since contributed news and features to a wide variety of publications, as well as producing and editing corporate magazines and papers. She is now researching and updating the archives at Sudeley Castle, on which this book is based. She has four grown-up children and lives with her artist husband in Winchcombe.

Acknowledgements

I would particularly like to thank Lady Ashcombe for permission to use the Emma Dent Diaries and all the plates in this book which have come from the Sudeley Castle archives. The cartoons were drawn by Emma Dent's sister, Marianne Brocklehurst.

Jean Bray
2004

ACKNOWLEDGEMENTS

FOREWORD

Anyone who comes to Sudeley Castle soon becomes aware of Emma Dent. Her hand is evident everywhere – in the Castle buildings, in its treasured and historical contents and in the gardens which she planned and loved so well. However, it seemed to me that everyone knew what Emma did and had done but that very little was known about her as a person.

This was so until some years ago when I decided to explore a pile of trunks and packing cases which had remained tucked away in the old 'Long Room' in the Castle, untouched for nearly a century. There I discovered the stored treasures of Emma Dent's life, an amazing collection of diaries, scrapbooks, letters, costumes and lace all of which we have since used to create at Sudeley a permanent exhibition of her life and times.

Most important of all in this collection of bygones were her detailed and lively diaries which vividly chronicled her time at Sudeley and showed her to be a vigorous and lively woman with a clear mind, a ready wit and a strong will.

These diaries have formed the basis for this book.

Elizabeth Ashcombe
Sudeley Castle

CHAPTER ONE

'I remember that summer morning – waking up and finding no-one there – for I slept in Father and Mother's room – and seeing there was no-one to talk to I amused myself by pinning the white curtains from within my little white bed – and pretending to be asleep when nurse came to dress me, and then I found the note they had left me hoping their absence had not disturbed my slumbers'.

Emma was four-years-old at the time and her father, John Brocklehurst, who headed the family silk business in Macclesfield, had taken advantage of the freedom to travel in Europe following the Napoleonic wars, to take his wife and elder daughter to visit some of the silk trading towns on the Continent.

'Baby Philip was a year old', Emma remembered. 'He was entrusted to the care of Aunt William at Tytherington, but when they returned from abroad, Father said he was over-fed, which was the cause of his having bad eyes, and we went to Buxton on his account. There I heard for the first time a Band of Music – from the high nursery window looking down upon the crescent, all the men in blue drapes – each

11

with their music on a stand before them – and the big drums. At first I was frightened – then it gradually became very pleasant to listen to'.

'It was then also that I was entrusted to walk alone sometimes, and I remember the awe with which I walked thro' a little gate and penetrated the depths of what appeared to me then to be a large mysterious wood. The rooks were cawing – the birds singing – I sat down to listen. I wanted so much to understand what they said and sang'.

The same curiosity prompted her, on their return home to Hurdsfield House, to dig up all the seeds she had recently planted in her own garden patch, to make sure they were growing, in spite of warnings from her three elder brothers, William, Henry and Peter.

Emma was fortunate to have been born into the large and wealthy Brocklehurst family, which in the nineteenth century, had established in Macclesfield one of the most important silk milling businesses in England, employing more than 8,000 hands at the height of its prosperity. Her grandfather, also called John Brocklehurst, had married a Cheshire heiress, Sarah Pownall, after starting the mills, and we are told 'he cared not for trade, but like the good squires of old sat in his chimney corner, entertained his friends and sought for nothing beyond his own and his neighbour's happiness'. It was under his industrious sons, John and Thomas that the silk business began to flourish.

John, Emma's father made the import of raw silk for the throwing mills his special study and he protested vigorously, both in and out of Parliament, when the advent of Free Trade in 1832 threatened the future of the Macclesfield mills. Later, when the silk trade was in the doldrums in the middle of the nineteenth century he spent £70,000 of his own money keeping his mills going and his workforce from starving, saying that he had made his money in Macclesfield, and if need be he would spend it there down to his last sixpence.

He and his wife, Mary, lived in the spacious Hurdsfield House, where Emma was born on the 5 March 1823. When Macclesfield first became enfranchised under the 1832 Reform Bill he was elected one of the town's first Members of Parliament, continuing the radical politics of his father, who had been a great admirer of Charles James Fox. This gave Emma her first chance to visit London and she was soon badgering her father – 'I think Mama is a very long time in making up her mind to go to London; I long to come and see you and the bazaars again' she wrote. 'Next Tuesday I shall be ten-years-old, I hope you will not forget to drink my health'.

Victorian girls were usually educated at home and taught by a resident governess. John and Mary Brocklehurst broke with this tradition first when they sent Emma's elder sister Anne to finish her education at Miss Green's school in Chester, where she was to die aged only sixteen from 'fever and mismanagement'. On the night before she died she was apparently moved from the school to lodgings in a sedan chair and 'carried upstairs by a man out of the street' – soon after she became delirious and the doctor administered laudanum. When her mother arrived with her own doctor Miss Green refused to take them to Anne until they threatened to call the police – they found her unconscious and she died a few hours afterwards.

Following this terrible tragedy Mary Brocklehurst was anxious that Emma should be taught at home, but her father had found an excellent tutor in London and in 1836 aged thirteen, Emma went to live with Senor Bruno, an elderly Italian grammarian and his daughters who, she said 'gave me all the education I ever had'. Her lessons included French, Italian and some German, as well as singing and music. Many years later she wrote nostalgically about her nights there, sleeping in a small iron bedstead, from which she would creep to stand at the window and watch the passers-by in the Euston Road.

She was even philosophical when her father decided she should miss one Christmas at home to continue with her studies, writing to her mother of the joys she would miss – 'Eating roast beef and plum pudding with old faces – joining in a merry dance and still more merry games at cards – and warbling and waltzing on uncarpeted boards until 2 o'clock in the morning . . . But I hope, my dear Mama, you will perceive that it will be for my real good to continue my studies in London until about the 20th of February, when Papa has promised I shall be conveyed home under the protection of one of my brothers'.

Life in London also had its compensations. There was great excitement on the evening before Queen Victoria's coronation, when her father arrived with tickets for Emma and her friend Jane Gaskell, to attend the ceremony.

'The next morning, long before it was light, we were at the gates waiting to go in with the first rush at eight o'clock, and good places we had', she wrote in her journal. 'Looking down the nave, on the side aisles where sat the Peers and Peeresses and the young and lovely Queen before the altar. I remember the crown catching in her hair at one part of the ceremony, when she had to take it off and place it on the altar, and how Lord Roll tripped up the steps as he went up to the throne to pay obeisance (he was very old and feeble) and how he fell a second time and then the Queen, with a natural impulse, rushed forward to assist him and the thunder of applause that followed . . . Then I shall never forget the "God save the Queen'." (Emma kept her Coronation ticket all her life and it is now in the Emma Dent Exhibition at Sudeley Castle).

Four years later, in 1841, she was presented at Court by Lady Stanley of Alderley, the wife of one of John Brocklehurst's Parliamentary colleagues. A friend of Emma's, General Clarke Kennedy, who was equerry to Prince Albert, promised to keep an eye on her during the ceremony and said he would be ready to pick her up if she fainted or became entangled in her long train. Apparently all went well, and she then enjoyed a coming-out party which was given for her by the Vallances – more family friends – in their Cavendish Square home.

Now she was both 'out' and accomplished Emma returned to Macclesfield to continue her music and languages and to teach her younger sister, Marianne. Nearly ten years Emma's junior, Marianne was the youngest of John and Mary Brocklehurst's six surviving children, and was already the family beauty. Emma had unfortunately inherited the worst features from both her parents – the drooping eyelids of the Brocklehursts, and the 'notable chin' and 'nutcracker' profile of the Coares. After she was married she was said by some to look like Marie Antoinette, a resemblance she enjoyed, particularly after Silvy, a Society photographer of the time, photographed her, handkerchief in hand with a prison background, in the style of Paul de la Roche's painting of the unfortunate queen.

For the time being however 'Life was carefree – driving, riding, hollering – lovers, friends, everything was "*couleur de rose*"' she said. 'The Polka then was all the rage and we danced it morning, noon and night'.

Nevertheless as a member of the Brocklehurst family, duty was never far behind and she soon entered with just as much enthusiasm into the 'poor peopling', which was then expected of girls of her age and class. On the first page of her 1844 pocket book she listed her sick visiting list as – 'one partial insanity, three dropsy and six consumption'. The same year she went into Hurdsfield Sunday School 'in fear and trembling' to take a class for the first time and she continued to be a Sunday School teacher for the rest of her life.

Although her family were Unitarians she became swept up in the evangelical religion which was a great force in the nineteenth century, and was known in the family as 'the little Methodist'. 'Theology was often discussed among us, but always in the most loving spirit', Emma recalled. 'Our father always told us to struggle after Truth, each for himself – that

Truth would prevail – he was much interested in Geology and Science, just then struggling into life – and he used to say that some of us might live to see Unitarianism preached in the Church of England'. Although Emma later lost some of her evangelical fervour, she kept her hatred of ritualism and the Catholic church.

In 1878, when she was in her fifties, she put together a family scrapbook in which she recorded some of the events of her early life and her happy and united family home. 'Father, though very severe and strict in all that concerned his children was so good – setting us such a bright example of rectitude, religion, industry and self-discipline. He was always temperate and sober – seemed never to rule us and yet always had us well in hand'. Emma was supposed to require 'talking to' sometimes. 'Then it was an awful moment when I was called into the 'little parlour' and a check given to my rather random ways – for I was rather too fond of fun and when young friends were staying with us I was a ringleader in little larks – innocent enough I believe – but dressing up for charades – 'midnight revels' in the smoking room with brothers, he thought required now and then the wet blanket. During these ordeals my courage was kept up by knowing my brothers were waiting for me in the passage to propose a ride, or walk, or game of billiards to put me in good spirits again – and in truth it did not take much to do it!'

'My mother too was always kind and gentle, wonderfully so – I never heard her say an unkind or sharp word to any of us', Emma wrote.

'All our uncles, cousins and brothers were alive in

those happy days'. Aunt and Uncle William lived at Tytherington. Aunt William and Emma's mother were sisters, William and John Brocklehurst, having followed their father's advice to 'wed riches', married the well-endowed Coare sisters, Anne and Mary. Uncle William, the elder brother, chose the law rather than the silk trade, and later extended the Brocklehurst's interests in Macclesfield by starting the Brocklehurst Bank in the town in 1816, in partnership with his brothers and his legal partner Robert Bagshaw.

He and Aunt William had no children of their own and adopted Emma's younger brother Philip when he was still quite young.

Aunt and Uncle Tom lived at The Fence with their ten children and he and his sons worked in the silk mills with Emma's father and brothers – 'all busy, useful, good men', Emma wrote. 'Mother and I did our best in keeping up pleasant cheerful society for them in the evenings. We had plenty of music, dancing, reading, games. Henry played the flute beautifully – we often sat up half the night trying over a fresh parcel of music from London. We roused William's ambitions and I undertook to teach him singing, but he didn't have the same talent as Henry in music'.

Nevertheless it was William, her eldest brother who took her to the Manchester Gentlemen's Concerts – 'Driving 20 miles there in the dear old pony carriage – no railways then – and often returning the same night, singing and joking all the way'.

By this time Emma had plenty of admirers, including Henry Beresford, cousin of the Marquess of Waterford, who had admired her driving skills with a four-in-hand while she was staying in Dublin, and after writing her amusing letters from Ireland, came to offer himself as a Valentine on Valentine's Day 1844. He, like many others, was turned away, until she met Robert Chester at a week long houseparty.

'Mr Robert Chester and I fell in love with one another and I accepted him', Emma recalled. 'To make a long, long story short, Father, aunts, uncles all objected. I could not go against them and for their dear sakes I gave up what I firmly believe was my greatest happiness'. (Years later he came to Cheltenham and walked among the Cotswold hills to see where Emma lived at Sudeley Castle and said to a mutual friend 'No home could be too beautiful for her.')

Emma never mentioned Robert Chester again and perhaps as an antidote for her broken heart the Brocklehursts arranged for her and her brother Henry to go on a European tour with Mr Osborne, who was then headmaster of Macclesfield Grammar School.

They travelled far and fast in those days of posting (travelling by stage coach) – Brussels, Cologne, Bonn, Coblenz and through Switzerland to Italy and back through France. 'Mr Osborne had but a short time for his travels', Emma wrote 'the cost of posting very considerable, making every hour precious, so we continued to see as much as possible in the shortest time and then posted on to somewhere else. We often travelled all night – but an hour or two's rest and a good breakfast refreshed me for a picture gallery or sightseeing'.

Emma returned with her mind a kaleidoscope of rocks and mountains, clouds, churches, paintings, statues, bronzes, gold and silver, changing carriages, jingling of bells, hunger, fatigue, thirst, fleas by dozens – 'everything charming and alarming at the same time'.

After travelling abroad together she and Mr Osborne became great friends and allies. He lent her books and encouraged her to discuss them, and both at home and during their travels he would select a subject for conversation which would be carried on for an evening, or a walk and kept to during the time agreed upon, 'which was excellent for rubbing up our wits' Emma said.

Much to her amusement he made her a member of his Pantagrealistical Society – the attributes for which were quick wittedness and a high degree of '*je ne sais quoi*'.

It was through Mr Osborne's friendship with the Dent family that in 1845 a newcomer was invited to join the Brocklehurst's annual grouse shooting party at Swythamley, Aunt William's country estate in Staffordshire. His name was John Coucher Dent, and he proved to be pleasant company, a good shot and, to the family's great interest, he was due to inherit a castle.

CHAPTER TWO

Sudeley Castle lies in a fold of the Cotswold hills, next to the town of Winchcombe and some eight miles north east of Cheltenham. Once a Royal residence and the home of Queen Katherine Parr, following its 'slighting' by order of Cromwell's Parliament in 1647, it had been little more than a romantic ruin for nearly 200 years, when John and William Dent, wealthy glovemakers from Worcester first caught sight of it while riding in the surrounding hills.

The bachelor Dent brothers had accumulated their wealth at a time when the glove industry was expanding and flourishing. Gloves were a major fashion article, in great demand and trade was buoyant until,like the Brocklehurst's silk business, it was threatened by the Free Trade Bill of 1832, which allowed fine quality French and Italian gloves to be legally imported into Britain for the first time, (although they had been smuggled in for many years). The Dents met the new challenge by improving the quality of their own gloves,and by opening up a warehouse in London to start a successful glove import and export business.

They were enthusiastic antiquarians and were looking for an interesting restoration project on which to spend their by then considerable fortune, when they saw Sudeley Castle and estate spread out below them and determined to acquire it. Fortunately Lord Rivers had already put the estate on the market and agreed to sell it to them in 1830, but they had to wait another seven years before they were able to buy the Castle itself and the remaining sixty acres from the Duke of Buckingham and Chandos. The Duke had purchased this from Lord Rivers in 1810 and tenanted it to a publican as 'The Castle Arms', with an eye on the tourist trade.

However, in 1837 Sudeley Castle and estate were united by the Dents and the work of restoration began. At that time only the north part of the outer court of the Castle was habitable and was then occupied by a tenant farmer. The remainder of the derelict buildings had been left to decay, while the neighbourhood builders picked over and plundered its stones.

The Dents, with the advice of their architect, Harvey Eginton of Worcester, began by restoring the Elizabethan ranges of the outer quadrangle built by the second Lord Chandos which, with the fifteenth century gatehouse, were still relatively intact. Their decision to leave the medieval buildings of the inner court – including the banqueting hall – in their state of picturesque ruin has been applauded by present day architects as showing a historical sense and a respect for the architectural nature of the buildings which was very rare in Victorian times, particularly among the 'nouveaux riches'.

The Dents' interest in Sudeley soon became an absorbing passion and they were determined to collect anything and everything that had a bearing on the history of the Castle. The famous Strawberry Hill Sale in 1842, when over 32 days Horace Walpole's celebrated Gothic collection came under the hammer, provided an opportunity for them to acquire some of the valuable Tudor treasures which furnish Sudeley today.

Their nephew, John Coucher Dent, who was then reading for the Bar in London, was sent to bid on their behalf.

He was the son of their brother Thomas – the only one of that generation of the Dent family to marry – Benjamin, the other brother having gone into the church. Thomas had stayed in the glove business with his father when John and William set up their own company and he had married Mary Coucher, the daughter of an old family friend. Both Thomas and Mary died while their sons, John and Martin, were still very young, and the two orphaned boys were educated and brought up by their Dent Uncles, who sent them both to Eton. John, usually known as John Coucher, to distinguish him from his Uncle John, went on to New College, Oxford and was called to the Bar in 1846, the year after he met Emma Brocklehurst. Martin was articled to a lawyer in Cirencester, but he 'played around', fell into low company and 'married beneath him' as a result of which he was disowned by the Uncles and went to Australia to seek his fortune. John Coucher was therefore being groomed to succeed to the Castle. He had never shown any interest in glove-making and when his Uncles, John and William Dent, decided to retire in 1845 they sold their glove business to John Derby Allcroft, the son of their partner, Jeremiah Macklin Allcroft, although they still kept their Worcester home at 34 Foregate Street and also kept control and received rent from their premises in Worcester and London.

The introduction of John Coucher Dent and the prospect of Sudeley Castle had caused a great flutter in the Brocklehurst family, and soon correspondence and invitations were being cordially exchanged between them and the Dents. Emma's parents with her sister Marianne and her governess were invited to stay at the Castle, and John Coucher Dent was being made welcome in Macclesfield.

'Aunt William called this morning and I believe she will wish a week with her at Tytherington towards the end of the month, a week also at the Fence and at Jordangate will be expected, so I hope you will prepare your wardrobe accordingly and put down amongst other items a *month at least*,' Emma's mother wrote to him.

Emma remained unperturbed by all the excitement. Having been prevented from marrying the man she loved, she was determined to devote her life to working among the poor and sick. She was already becoming skilled at wound dressing 'without flinching' and in teaching blind children, having learnt the system from Mr Moon, who had invented a raised letter system similar to Braille.

Inexplicably however, she changed her mind when in the following year the first Brocklehurst family link was broken by the death of Aunt William, who caught cold during the damp bad weather of early January while superintending some tree cutting on the drive at Tytherington. Pleurisy with great pain set in and she died within a week. After her death Emma stayed behind in the desolate house to look after Uncle William and her brother Philip. 'Aunt William was very beautiful in death' she recalled, 'holding in her hands some exquisite and rare white lilies which she had been anxiously watching and waiting to flower'.

By her death-bed Emma resolved to marry John Coucher Dent. 'I know not why in losing her I should have changed my mind', she said, later claiming that John came to Tytherington and made her promise to be his wife and with the 'unlimited approbation' of the elders of both families, Emma and John Coucher Dent became engaged.

The Brocklehurst family's enthusiasm for the match was overshadowed for a time when Emma's mother, still greatly shocked by the death of her sister, became dangerously ill herself. For nearly a month Emma nursed her devotedly both by day and all night – strong coffee and Disraeli's novel *Coningsby*, which had just been published at the time, keeping her awake till dawn.

With her mother's recovery, plans for the wedding went ahead – 'everything going as merrily as wedding bells,' wrote John, enjoying the charm of writing 'My own Emma' and 'My Tic-a-Toc' (a pet name for her from a song she used to sing).

Then 'Shout ye glades of Hurdsfield, break forth into singing ye meads of Tytherington, re-echo the glad notes ye knights of Herridge', because Emma's father was going to meet his Uncles to talk over the momentous question of the marriage settlement.

They wrote to each other every day of their six months engagement – except by agreement on Sundays – Sunday being a particularly busy day for Emma with her Sunday School classes. She kept all John's letters for thirty years before deciding to dispose of them. 'Six months correspondence in their small envelopes according to the fashion of the day – with blue-red stamps so much prized by the stamp collector. It would be sad for them to fall into the fire as lumber – those good honest love letters, better perhaps that they should have a Christian burial from my hand'.

Meanwhile events outside the family were dominated by the election, and political fever was running high that summer of 1847. Emma's father was again head of the poll in Macclesfield but a 'wretched' Radical called Williams had replaced Grimsditch as the other Member for the town. Emma was disgusted with her maverick brother Peter, who had not only voted for Williams but had also made an oration from a cart to a delighted mob. It turned out that he had done it to annoy Uncle William and his partner Bagshaw to whose legal firm Peter was articled at the time. John Coucher Dent reported that her father's friend, Craven Berkeley, the Liberal MP for Cheltenham had been beaten by the Conservatives (although the result was later overturned following allegations of bribery and corrupt practice).

September came and the 'settlements' were settled –

£30,000 on each – the dresses made and the ring fitted. 'The intended marriage of Miss Brocklehurst, the accomplished daughter of our highly esteemed representative John Brocklehurst Esq. MP with John Coucher Dent Esq. Barrister-at-law, nephew and heir presumptive of John Dent Esq. of Sudeley Castle, created much interest in a locality wherein the family of the fair bride have been so long resident and are so justly esteemed by all classes of their neighbours', reported the *Macclesfield Chronicle*. 'The active exertions of the young lady herself in furthering the education of the children of the poor, aided by her personal superintendence of weekly and Sunday schools in the locality, have not only endeared her to all parents and children benefited by her praiseworthy efforts, but must render her removal from the vicinity of Macclesfield a loss not soon to be supplied'.

On their wedding day, 16 September, crowds lined the road between Hurdsfield House and the parish church at Prestbury to watch the bridal procession. 'The bride was attired in rich white-watered silk with flounces of Honiton lace looped up with bouquets of orange flowers; a wreath of orange blossom on her head and a handsome veil to correspond' and she also wore the magnificent diamond necklace and brooch which were a wedding present from the Dent Uncles. Her seven bridesmaids in 'white tarlatane muslin dresses with pink silk visits and white transparent bonnets with pink flowers' included her sister Marianne and two friends, Mary Worthington and Ann Fielden, who were later to marry two of her brothers. John's Uncle Ben – the Rev. Benjamin Dent

MA – performed the wedding service which was followed by 'an elegant *dejeuner-a-la-fourchette*' at the bride's home.

'At three o'clock the happy couple entered a travelling carriage drawn by four greys for Rowsley, near Chatsworth, *en route* for Italy, amid the encouraging huzzas of the assembled guests'. Only her mother could not bear to watch Emma go, and they parted in tears at the door on the staircase in the front hall – neither of them realising that this was to be their final farewell.

Then followed a stormy journey over the Buxton Moor. Such a boisterous wind greeted them on their arrival at the Cat and Fiddle in Rowsley that Martin the courier's umbrella was blown away like a balloon, followed by Mary the maid's basket of cake and brandy bottle.

Writing home from Europe to her mother Emma described the contents of her little carpet bag, which was being continually unpacked as they were '*toujours en route*' and it was stuffed as full as possible – pair of slippers, dressing gown, two pairs of stockings, boots, a dress rolled up, a Bible, a bottle of Maccassar oil, crumpled collar and mouchoir de poche.'

'We have been married more than a fortnight and we draw breath every Thursday with 'many happy returns of the day'. We get on admirable as Palabot would say. Martin, the courier, is an excellent manager, looks after us as children – takes care we are not too late for the trains – keeps the provision basket well supplied and greets me with fruit or flowers every morning. Mary, the maid, is lost in amazement at everything and makes herself as needed'.

They honeymooned for six months in a Europe split by revolution. 'Throughout Europe it was a winter of great political excitement', Emma wrote. 'We were fortunate to be in the thick of it, yet always escaping a few hours before the actual revolution broke out – thus while at Palermo we accomplished our perilous expedition to Calatafimi (where we experienced the last earthquake). Going on to Messina on the *Nettuno* in a gale of wind, with thunder and lightning which the Italians would never have faced had it not been for the necessity of getting certain military men to Messina, where a revolution was also hourly expected. The following day Palermo was in revolt – out hotel in Messina was guarded by soldiers – Catania was also in revolt – but we had no idea of danger and when the weather permitted, for it rained every day for a week, we took delightful walks and expeditions.'

'Our courier, however, was glad to hurry us on board the first steamer that touched at Messina, so we went to Malta to escape the revolt. In truth when we returned a fortnight or three weeks later we were shocked to see the havoc done by the insurgents – our hotel riddled like perforated cardboard and the windows of our rooms all smashed.'

'At Malta we were welcomed by the officers of the *Trafalgar* – they made our stay most delightful, getting up picnics and all manner of amusements for us. The *Trafalgar* was considered a fine old man-of-war in those days. Lieutenant Arkwright was an immense favourite – then there was Onslow, Miller and Thomas – they all told me their love stories' Emma wrote.

They had travelled back as far as Naples when bad news came from Hurdsfield. 'Our dear Mother not well – her strength failing fast'. Both her father and Marianne wrote telling them that there was no time for them to travel back from Europe, but they had taken places and were sailing home when they heard the sad news of her death on 7 February 1848.

'The moon shone on the sea. I knelt all night at the cabin window weeping as the porpoises played in the moonshine' Emma wrote. 'It was a wonderful and awfully beautiful scene. I always associate those effects with that sorrow, as I do the early singing of birds and the twittering of sparrows among the ivy with the time of her recovery the year before.'

As there was now no longer any urgency for them to return home, they decided to stay on in Rome, and only when the Italian revolution began to make it unsafe for travel at the end of April did they sail for France, where they found conditions there even more disturbed. 'Every place in the Malle Poste taken for the next fortnight – between the two revolutions we were in despair how to proceed' Emma recalled. 'Then two places fell vacant if we would go on that same day – we left maid and courier to travel by diligence – and travelled on by Malle Poste to Paris where we arrived on 6th May at four o'clock in the morning, not having had one night in bed since the 28th April.'

On 18 May they came home to Hurdsfield. William met them at Chelford, the nearest railway station, with the pony carriage, leaving the servants and luggage to follow, and Emma was faced with the reality of her mother's death – 'It seemed as if my tears would never stop', she said. 'Each fresh face opened the floodgates afresh'.

CHAPTER THREE

In August 1848 Emma and John settled into their first home – Severn Bank – a house set amongst the woods and high above the banks of the River Severn near Severnstoke in Worcestershire, which they leased from the Coventry family. Emma loved the woods there and the large bow window in the drawing room, which seemed almost to hang over the River Severn and looked out over the plain to the Malvern Hills.

'Our days at Severn Bank flowed quietly on', she wrote in her journal. 'We were kindly received by our county neighbours. Every week we went to Worcester to see the good old Uncles, or they were with us, on their way to and from Sudeley. I occupied myself in books and works and music – taking lessons in singing from John Barnett and constantly practising with Mr Coventry, who was devoted to his flute'. Soon her grand piano arrived. (It had been made originally for Queen Victoria, who had returned it to Broadwoods because it was maple and not rosewood.)

'We had a succession of visitors – and there were

many pleasant things to do', Emma wrote, 'but Severn Bank was a quiet place and my old journal has a melancholy ring of missing the old merry life of Hurdsfield, especially the cheerful evenings with my brothers. Then I turned my mind to the poor. I took an interest in the schools and started a large pence club among them.

Two of Emma's brothers were married by this time, to two of her bridesmaids. John Fielden of Todmorden, a Radical MP for Oldham and one of the leading campaigners for the Ten Hours Movement for reducing working hours in industry, was a great friend of Emma's father and Ann, his second daughter, and Emma became friends. Emma said she was a fascinating girl, but in some ways delicate, and had 'habits of indolence and indulgence which were encouraged by her doctors and were to lead to much sorrow and mischief in her later life.' Ann had stayed on at Hurdsfield for several days after being a bridesmaid at the wedding, much to Henry Brocklehurst's delight. 'He was so handsome and warm-hearted and gay, no-one could have refused him – much less Ann Fielden' said Emma and they were married while Emma and John were away on their honeymoon tour of Europe. Once again the Brocklehurst family welcomed the link to another great trading dynasty, for the Fieldens of Todmorden were among the largest cotton manufacturers in Lancashire at the time.

The following year William. Emma's eldest brother, married Mary Worthington, another of her bridesmaids. William had a house built for them at Butley to escape from his father's plan that they should move in with him at Hurdsfield, so that Mary could be in charge of Marianne, the household and the domestics.

At Severn Bank Emma and John settled down to live the life of the county set – with dinner parties, balls, summer evenings under the cedars and on the water at Pirton, days at the races (which Emma hated), hunting and shooting – but she was still homesick for Hurdsfield. 'I was always sad to return to Severn Bank', she recalled. 'It was so cheerful among my brothers and cousins in Macclesfield and I used to think the Dents never had family jokes as we had'.

Then John had his first bad attack of gout – perhaps the pipe of port which Uncle Ben had given them as a wedding present had not been such a good idea – and future attacks were to punctuate their married life.

'John laid up with gout and rheumatism caught by fishing in the Isbourne – very bad times these' wrote Emma, 'very bad when a young wife has to face gout in her husband for the first time. *Le vin est verse, il faut le boire*'.

John also proved to have the choleric temperament which so often accompanies gout, and there was gossip and rumours among both friends and servants that he was often violent and beat her. Emma was reputed to be very angry when she heard this, and reading between the lines of her own account of her life, she seems to have suffered more from 'many unkind and hasty words' than from physical violence, but she was dismayed by his rages, taking refuge in her work among the poor, which she claimed helped her to forget her unhappiness.

Her other great consolation was her new horse, Black Prince, who would only let her ride him. He threw everyone else who mounted him, including the groom and Marianne, which Emma said made her rather proud.

As their restoration of Sudeley Castle continued the Dent Uncles enjoyed using it as a background for lavish entertaining, and in March 1851 Uncle William, having been appointed High Sheriff of Gloucestershire, used the start of the Gloucester Assizes to put on a day of 'unbounded hospitality'. 'Oh what breakfasting and lunching and dinnering went on that day who can tell', Emma reported.

The Cheltenham Examiner gave its own fulsome report of the event, beginning with the breakfast. 'The well filled board was first spread at Sudeley Castle, the picturesque and romantic residence of the High Sheriff, where in a spacious and elegant marquee raised in the 'pleasance' . . . at nine o'clock a party of about two hundred guests, comprising many friends from Worcestershire and most of the farmers in the neighbourhood, sat down and partook of the good fare provided for them.' Breakfast concluded, a procession formed to escort the High Sheriff to Cheltenham *en route* for Gloucester. 'Proceeded by the javelin men in their gay liveries of blue and silver came the elegant carriage of the high Sheriff drawn by four splendid grey horses, followed by the family four-in-hand, about two hundred horsemen, two abreast ,and ten carriages containing private friends'. On arrival at Cheltenham an abundant luncheon, crowned by a baron of beef weighing 275 lbs was served in the

Town Hall, together with wines of the finest vintage from the cellars of the Plough. The same evening, following the opening of the Assizes in Gloucester more substantial dinners were served at the Bell Hotel and the King's Head.

The Reverend Francis Edward Witts, then Vicar of Stanway, commented rather acidly in his Diary after the event. 'All this is a bad precedent as regards future holders of the office. Much was the excess of those regaled at the High Sheriff's expense, and many the midnight stragglers wending their way home after copious libation.'

Emma considered Uncle William to be the jolliest of the Uncles, and in May that year he joined her and John at Long's Hotel in Bond Street for a few weeks in London to see the Great Exhibition. 'A sight it certainly was which we have never seen surpassed in any of our foreign wanderings', Emma wrote. She enjoyed sightseeing with Uncle William – 'the type of perfect English squire, with a childlike relish for the sights and sounds of the capital.'

She and John returned to London for another visit to the Great Exhibition on 6 October when 1700 people attended, which was thought to be a good number. However their main reason for being in London was for Emma to consult a doctor 'in the hope of getting into stronger health – for it was a great grief to have no children', she said.

Emma loved children and as it was she had to make do by borrowing her nephews and nieces whenever she could. At Severnstoke she enjoyed playing with the large family of Philpott children at the Rectory. 'What scenes of gypsies and robbers we used to get up to in the Severn Bank woods', she reminisced. 'A great trick was to dress up a figure to represent myself and pretend to be sitting on the battlements at the top of the house, then disappear the same moment the figure fell over into the garden'.

Bessie Calrow, one of several girls who described Emma as their 'Fairy Godmother' remembered expeditions in the woods. 'And just when we were feeling rather tired we came suddenly upon a fire, with a gypsy kettle and welcome tea ready. Sometimes an old woman was bending over the fire in a large bonnet and red cloak and we were half frightened and clung together, when a laughing face would look out at us from under the bonnet and we saw it was our hostess who had slipped away when we were all busy gathering blackberries.'

However, it was her younger sister, Marianne who was Emma's favourite companion. Now that she was of marriageable age she was already attracting a number of admirers – all of whom she rejected. They included Jerry Allcroft, who was now running the Dent glovemaking business, and the one most favoured by her father – Heathcote Amory, the MP for Tiverton. Three of the rest became baronets, 'but she was not for marrying and they were allowed to pass on without any hesitation on her part'.

John Dent was very fond of his young sister-in-law and in February 1852 he and Emma decided to take her on a European tour with them, giving Emma an escape from 'keys, cupboards and domestic troubles'. They landed in Boulogne and went from there to Paris where Marianne thought the Palais Royale by gaslight was simply fairyland – then on to Lyons, Valence and a 'charming' expedition down the Rhône in a steamer, although it was 'cold beyond description'.

By the beginning of May they were in Venice, having visited most of the Italian cities, including Rome, on the way. John was laid up with a bad attack of gout and Emma and Marianne amused themselves by buying photographs then taking a gondola to every scene, comparing the view with the picture, to impress it deeply on their minds.

On their return it was Emma's turn to be ill. 'I suffered very much indeed from my heart – frightful spasms which held me down sometimes for twenty minutes, so that I could not move', she wrote. 'The first I had was in my sleep and I dreamt that Death came with his dart – touched my heart and I woke in the acutest pain. I was ordered iron in quantities, but I was very ill and chilled and I remember how the warmth of the sun and the beauty of the Severn Bank roses contrasted and jarred with my morbid feelings'.

However, she soon recovered both health and spirits and was up playing billiards all evenings with Henry and Marianne – winning a sovereign from Henry and beating Marianne twice and 'unable to sleep for the triumph and excitement.'

That Autumn John's brother, Martin, appeared from Australia – broken in health, out of pocket and anxious to be reconciled to his family. Emma was glad to welcome the 'poor broken down wanderer' to Severn Bank, where Uncle William Dent came at once to see him – their first meeting after Martin's unfortunate marriage, which had led to the family rift and his long separation. Then Emma took him to see Uncle John in Worcester and all were reconciled.

Although Martin claimed to be a woman hater, following his wife's desertion, nobody cared for a lame dog like Emma and he was soon telling her all his troubles. His descriptions of life in Australia she said were just like those in Charles Reade's book *It is Never Too Late to Mend*.

Martin's wife had been seduced away by a man who had vowed to do so in revenge. Shortly before she left him their small child had died – hundreds of miles from a clergyman, he himself had had to read her burial service. Following this double blow, he had lived a vagabond life for some years before hearing rumours of gold strikes near Melbourne, where he was one of the first prospectors on the scene, until he was forced by consumption to give up mining and return to England.

Meanwhile, in November 1852 all England was mourning the death of the great hero, the Duke of Wellington, and John and Emma decided to go to London for his State Funeral on 18 November. On arrival they found there was not a bed to be had in the city, but the Vallance family made room for Emma in 35 Cavendish Square and John went to his friend, Mr. Franks. By six o'clock the following morning they were at the Conservative Club – 'It was very cold sitting and waiting at the open window for so many hours on that November morning – but the sun shone bright and warm rays fell on the procession as it slowly and mournfully passed down St James's Street', Emma recorded. 'It was a day of real hero worship such as we shall never see again'.

She was still disenchanted with her own lot. 'Very full of good resolves and fired with great ambition to do something great and very good', she wrote. 'I mourn that my days pass so unprofitably and in such small insignificant acts – chiefly among the poor and sick. I should feel happier if I could only believe my life, my present life might be preparing me for something worthier in the years to come'.

In January 1854 the River Severn which was the background to their home at Severn Bank froze over for the first time for sixteen years. 'When the thaw came on 8 January the noise of the ice breaking and rushing past was very strange and impressive', Emma said. On many other occasions the Severn flooded and they would have to go to church by boat, rowing over the fields and hedges.

But the main excitement that January was the election. John had been scampering round the county campaigning for Sir William Hicks Beach, who was standing for the first time for East Gloucestershire and on 14 January he returned, flushed with victory, from Gloucester to report a majority of 1019 in favour of the Conservatives. (Emma would have been amused to know that two generations later her great niece, Marjorie, would marry Sir William's great grandson, Viscount Quenington).

The Dents decided to celebrate the Tory triumph with a political ball at Sudeley Castle – the famous Blue Ball – and as neither of the Uncles were well enough, John was put in charge of both organising and hosting the event.

The Cheltenham Examiner reported that 'The total number present was not far short of 600 and for their accommodation a large temporary building was erected in the space which, centuries ago, formed the great banqueting hall of the Castle – the supper room was constructed in a similar manner in the pleasance – and both communicated with each other and different parts of the castle by means of passages and corridors erected for the occasion'.

Emma, writing to Uncle John, who had been forbidden by his doctors to attend the Ball, was full of its success. 'Nothing could possibly have gone off better. There was not one contretemps and I never saw 500 and more people look so happy. The castle was well lighted up and they rambled through the rooms and looked at the pictures and the marbles with great pleasure . . . the ballroom looked extremely pretty, and the night being so quiet the candles were not blown out as we expected . . . John says 398 sat down to supper the first time and the consumption of wine was 35–40 dozen . . . There was a tent erected for the men to smoke in and after supper if there was the slightest appearance of intoxication the individual was smuggled off into this self-same tent – so that everyone was astonished at the sobriety of the affair.'

'They were not all gone before seven o'clock next morning and those of the party staying in the castle who happened to be in bed before that time said that they were constantly disturbed by people going into their room and looking at them in bed. It is reported that three people were seen at once in Mr and Mrs Hookey's room – and that they were taken for Henry VIII and Anne Boleyn!'

'Your and Uncle William's busts bore blue round their necks and we had some serious thoughts of putting some yellow on Cromwell . . . John got from Cheltenham some of those things for fires used in streets when they are laying down gas and they lighted up the road under the walnut trees and the quadrangle and had a very good effect . . . Smith at the Turnpike cleared five pounds and sported a blue flag. A great many men played at cards in the library and tea was going on for ages in the billiard room . . . Altogether the people never had such a treat and it will never be forgotten.'

The Blue Ball was held in February 1854 and the following April a beautiful comet appeared over the Malvern Hills, but this was looked on as a sign of the war which was then starting in the Crimea. General Bell, a great friend of the Dent Uncles, who Emma considered an honorary uncle, had two sons serving in the Army and both were off to fight. Montagu (Monty) was at a Malta so crowded with military that the officers had to sleep on the floor. He had been ordered to Varna and his wardrobe restricted by order to three shirts and six pairs of socks. His brother Ned's ship had reached Gibraltar. It was the end of the year before troops landed in the Crimea and the battle of Alma was reported as a 'glorious success', although 2,000 English and French were killed. *The Times* reported that 'the officers of the 23rd were all killed but three, of whom the senior was Captain Bell.' 'His poor old father, the General was nearly beside himself with joy and fear that the wording might be incorrect', Emma said.

Emma's own contribution to the war effort was to send off a parcel to Florence Nightingale in Scutari hospital consisting of 100 shirts, mitts and comforters. 'There was not much else I could do for those in that dreadful war', she said 'so I wrote all the little news I could collect to any officers I knew of'.

The end of the year was to prove a sad one with the death of Uncle William Dent at his house in Foregate Street, Worcester, aged seventy-one. He had been ill for some time and the doctors said his heart was worn out. They brought him back to Sudeley to be buried. 'They are making a vault' Emma reported. In excavating it they discovered a skeleton with the remains of a handsome sword beside it, and an important lead coffin, raised at head and feet and ribbed down the centre. This was opened in the presence of Mr Edmund Brown, Mr Pruon, Dr Newman and Mr Woodcock and the bones inside were all in perfect condition, but there was no inscription of any kind.

'October 19th was the day of our good Uncle's funeral', Emma wrote. 'It was fine, but cold. I had a fire in the 'Queen's room' and sat there alone.' (Women did not attend funerals at that time). 'The scene from the window was very sad and impressive as the procession wended its way into the little side chapel. When they entered the chapel I opened the Chandos room window which enabled me to hear every word of the Burial Service, which was impressively read by Mr Harvey; the service seemed to take us to the very gates of heaven and there we left him'.

The year 1855 began with 'my husband wishing I may be much happier than in the last,' said Emma. The Crimean War continued to be the all absorbing subject and the correspondent of *The Times* was said to be in disgrace for repeating too freely what he had heard at Lord Raglan's table.

General and Mrs Bell and Una Hassall, who was engaged to Monty Bell, were staying at Severn Bank with John and Emma and enjoying a week of festivities in aid of the Patriotic Fund and 'all the time poor Monty was dead in his Crimean grave', Emma said. 'On 26th January when they were all with us after a ball at Upton the news came – before they were down – it was an awful morning' she recalled. 'The Irish warmth of heart broke out into the wildest wailing – poor Mrs Bell tearing her hair – Una the picture of despair. It seemed to help us realise the horrors of war.'

This was soon to be followed by their own tragedy, when John's brother, Martin died aged only thirty-four. Since his return from Australia he had been progressing round the English seaside in the hope of recovering from his consumption. Only the year before, Emma had taken him to Scarborough for a month in an attempt to nurse him back to health. Now he was in Torquay where Emma, John and Marianne rushed to his bedside.

'His life hangs on a thread', Emma wrote. 'What a sad picture of humanity is a dying bed scene – the bottles of medicine – the dainty food and drink prepared, but left untouched – soft footsteps, subdued voices, anxious faces. – Poor Martin, sometimes he seemed quite dead, tho' propped up in bed, with his head hanging forward – forehead and nose like marble, eyelids blue and his red hair long and straggling, reminding me most forcibly of the German type by some of the Old Masters of 'Dead Christ'. He is very patient and assented to my telling his Uncles that he is resigned, trusting in his Redeemer for salvation'. As he died the snow fell and lay on the ground outside – a most unusual sight for Torquay.

Martin was buried at Sudeley. 'It seemed but yesterday I was watching him standing over the grave of his Uncle William', Emma recalled. 'And now like a shadow he has himself followed.

Now that he is gone how little we seem to have left to remind us of his very eventful life. The portrait of General Wolfe by Sir Joshua Reynolds in the Library was purchased because of its extraordinary likeness to him'. She also kept the first daguerreotypes of aborigines ever brought to England – 'a few nuggets of gold of his own finding' – his permit to dig, and the skull of a native woman who was killed in an affray with an English party – all of which were later mounted in the museum which she was to start at the castle.

The restoration work there was still continuing. The outbuildings and sheds which had extended across the second quadrangle were being pulled down and new stables planned in the old Dungeon Tower. Emma was against this improvement, but she was even more desperately opposed to the restoration of the Chapel, which was soon to be taken in hand by the architect Mr George Gilbert Scott, who had already gained a considerable reputation in restoring churches.

'I am very anxious Sudeley Chapel should not be restored, contrary to the opinion of all good people' Emma said. 'In my anxiety I was so bold as to write to Ruskin for his opinion which came today in a very interesting letter. He recommended no restoration, a pile of mossy stones a fitter monument for Queen Katherine Parr than the most gorgeous church that wealth could erect – alas, my wish, even backed by Ruskin goes for nothing'.

In June Mr Gilbert Scott himself arrived to discuss the restoration. 'It was an anxious morning', Emma reported 'for I somehow still clung to the hope that even at the eleventh hour it might be averted. I was so sorry for Mr Scott, for I could see he was puzzled to know what to do for the best – and grieved to give the order to scrape the walls and denude them of their exquisite greys and moss and roses – and wallflowers and elder trees'.

Emma had already paid her own last emotional visit to the ruined Chapel before the work began – 'the baby breezes blow gently in thro' the old broken windows – the jackdaws chatter on the pinnacles, then dart in and out among the ruins – the air is full of the scent of wallflowers never will this little Chapel be holier to me than now – the dead below – heaven above – God in everything – peace around – the last bee of the day comes murmuring in – a sudden gust of wind sounds like an organ note – then all again is silent – the bright blue sky deepens into purple – emblem of the change coming on all I esteem and revere so much here – a thousand holy thoughts, not unmixed with sorrow, well up in soul and mind as I sit and contemplate the past and future'.

Earlier they had opened Katherine Parr's vault and found everything in place since it had been closed thirty years earlier. They also found three skulls in the Chandos coffin and many bones and were surprised that all the monumental remains were in such good condition.

Her sister, Marianne had recently taken up

photography, which was still in its infancy, and was called in to help record the ruins on film before she and Emma took their usual summer holiday together in August, while the men were shooting. This year they went to Wales for a time of fishing (another of Marianne's enthusiasms), photography and 'unalloyed felicity' until John joined them at Llandudno and did his best to convince them that the hotel and many other things which they had enjoyed were bad, and impositions.

Emma was trying to persuade him to buy a large house called the Mythe, so that they could feel more settled as they were only renting Severn Bank on a six-monthly lease, and she was afraid they might be turned out at any time if it was needed by its owner, the young Lord Coventry.

However, before this could happen, Uncle John Dent was taken ill. He was on his way to Sudeley from Worcester when, according to his obituary, he took cold 'which superinduced a malady the results of which were fatal'. Emma and John were with him at Sudeley.

'The poor old man breathed his last on the 8th October in the evening at half past seven, in the room next to ours', Emma recalled. 'It was inexpressibly awful that waiting and watching, hour after hour, feeling that nothing can be done and that the ear is closed to sound as the eye to seeing, yet the heart is still beating. Saunders his faithful old man servant and I were alone with him when all was still'.

With Uncle John's death, at the age of seventy-eight, John Coucher inherited not only Sudeley Castle, but also the considerable Dent fortune (Uncle Ben, the clergyman having died earlier in 1850) and with no surviving relatives of his own, it was Emma's father and brother William who joined him as chief mourners at the funeral of the 'good old man'.

Emma once again watched the funeral procession from the window of the small crimson room in the castle. 'It was a beautiful day, so fine and bright as he would have wished it', she wrote 'and when the mourners returned John and I were left alone in the world – the last of his name, the last of his family'.

CHAPTER FOUR

It was the following Spring before Emma and John Dent moved their home from Severn Bank to Sudeley Castle. On 19 April 1856 Emma recorded: 'Everything being packed up and off, John followed on his favourite beautiful chestnut, kissing his hand to me as he trotted on – Pincher barking with his usual delight at accompanying a horse and his master'.

The next day it was Emma's turn to make her final departure. 'I went down to the village, the school and into the woods – those beautiful woods full of singing birds and wild flowers where I have spent my happiest hours', she wrote, adding somewhat hastily, 'the next happiest to those with the poor' . . . 'The sun shone very brightly all day, everything seemed to welcome me to my new home at beautiful Sudeley.'

However, before taking on their new responsibilties, Emma had been able to persuade John to go north to Macclesfield for Christmas and the New Year. Ann and Henry wanted them to come to the christening of their second son – Henry Dent Brocklehurst – and Emma welcomed the chance to spend Christmas with her family for the first time since their marriage. Previously they had always been expected to join the Dent Uncles at Worcester.

There was also the opportunity to enjoy her affectionate friendship with Sam Fielden, Ann's brother and now the head of the Fielden family's cotton business in Todmorden. Sam had often been a guest at Severn Bank, usually joining one of John's shooting parties and he had begun interesting her in politics by frequent invitations to attend debates in the House of Commons when she was in London.

That Christmas season he hosted a dance with an Arabian Nights theme and, much to everyone's amazement gas was introduced into his home at Centre Vale for the one evening to light the event. Emma was notably his favourite dancing partner and the following afternoon they spent together, attending a service at the Unitarian Chapel before going for a long walk across the moors. She tore the next page from her journal before mentioning another very happy evening on New Year's Eve when 'we were all like so many children and had a grand game of pretend siege – half of us in the dining room, and half out, wishing to come in.'

The next weekend she and Sam rode to Stoodley Pike – his favourite place high among the moors in the Upper Calder Valley, where he was planning to rebuild the moortop monument, which commemorated peace after war. She later gave £10 towards his rebuilding fund, saying 'I had an idea I should one day like to be buried there – that wild situation among the bleak moors of Yorkshire greatly took my fancy'.

THE LADY OF SUDELEY

For her birthday in March Sam gave her a beautiful miniature of Charles I by Rochard and inscribed on the back 'A true friend – thankful for many words of kindness – begs Mrs Dent to accept the miniature herewith as a humble contribution to the furnishings of Katherine Parr's room' (where it still hangs on the wall today). Emma said it cost £10 and Sam joked that it had been bought with self-denial money from cigars.

It is interesting to speculate how this relationship might have developed had Emma not been very conscious of her duty to her husband and above all to Sudeley. She and John had already had some long and serious talks over the past – ending, she said, in many good and noble resolutions for the future. But she still wrote rather enigmatically in her journal of 'the first wild bursting of the heart to flower and its cramping, crushing afterwards'.

At Sudeley Mr Gilbert Scott, the architect, had returned and was consulting with John again about moving the stables. He was against the ruins being touched and suggested they should be put in the old kitchen garden. Emma had persuaded him to leave the silica and the angels on the chapel wall 'unscraped' as an experiment and was pleased that he liked her suggestion of using arches to join the small side chapel to the main building, and was complimentary about the altar cloth she had designed and was embroidering, giving her advice on ways to improve the drapery on the angels.

There was still much to be done in the interior of the Castle. Mr Moxon came from London and decorating decisions were made – blue for the library, grey and cord for the dining room and oak for the upstairs dining room. Emma and Marianne decided to decorate the Chinese room themselves, which took two or three days hard work – papering and patching – for the paper proved to be too short, necessitating cutting extra pieces out and pasting them at the bottom to make it long enough. They took it in turns to go up the ladder and enjoyed arranging the colours for the door and the other paintwork.

The Uncles' old servants had been pensioned off and a fresh set employed. Elizabeth Bayliss, who had been Emma's personal maid and her constant companion since she joined the Dent's household in 1852, came with her to Sudeley and also took over the duties of housekeeper.

Victorian women were, among their other attributes, great improvers and Emma lost no time in collecting a class of young girls to attend at the Castle every Sunday. Her original idea had been to teach them religion, but this was soon extended to history and a 'little summing and writing', and, most important of all in her opinion, cutting out and sewing, for she found that the Winchcombe girls were 'lamentably ignorant in the use of the needle'.

Winchcombe at that time was a small Cotswold town of some two and a half thousand inhabitants. John Oakey, who was later to become Emma's builder, says in his book *Reminscences of Winchcombe* that 'The town had changed little since two centuries earlier – at the time of the failure of the tobacco growing enterprise and the damaging of the Castle by Parliamentary troops – Samuel Pepys had described it as a 'miserable poor place'. In the days before the motor car it was isolated by the barrier of Cleeve Hill and the main movements, social and industrial, which concerned much of the rest of England, had had little effect on Winchcombe'.

Most people in the town were employed on the land or in the four corn mills. There were also three small paper mills on the Isbourne, and a tannery. A coach came from Broadway twice a week, changing horses at the George Hotel and then going on to Cheltenham, but the townspeople thought nothing of walking to Cheltenham, and men used to walk from Broadway to Winchcombe to work and vice versa.

By June it was time for the Dent's first great 'sup-up' at Sudeley. Three hundred children from the Winchcombe Sunday and Day schools, Emma's own class of young women, and some of the estate workers were invited.

'The procession with all the banners and our arrangements of flowers and other devices was really beautiful', Emma reported. 'All was new to the children and they were very happy. John looked after the farmers and their wives – starting games and administering negus (a drink made of port, sugar, lemon and spice) etc., for we had climbing poles, balloons, sack races and every other amusement suitable for the occasion'. Emma gave Peace medals to commemorate the end of the Crimean War, to the older children, teachers and guests.

In contrast their next big event was the British Association meeting in Cheltenham, for which they collected a large house party. The British Association for the Advancement of Science had been founded in

1831 and its aims of stimulating scientific inquiry and spreading scientific knowledge greatly appealed to Emma's curious nature, although she admitted finding the paper on the Correlation of Physical Force 'rather hard to grasp'.

On the final day of the meeting all the delegates came to Sudeley in eight carriages, omnibuses and on horseback. Mr Norwood read a paper on the Castle's history – 'then we rambled thro' the rooms – they were all hungry and enjoyed their 'victuals' before going on to see the excavations at Hailes Abbey and to visit Stanway and Toddington.'

Agnes Strickland, author of *The Lives of the Queens of England* was among the Dent's house party for the Association meeting and Emma managed to persuade her to help with ideas for a Tudor entertainment which she was planning.

Another favourite new venture was her Fife and Drum Band. After hearing one at Macclesfield in the summer she had been determined to start one in Winchcombe,and by the end of the year they were playing well enough to perform in the Castle quadrangle for the first time, in honour of Major Ned Bell, the Crimean hero.

Soon it was Christmas again and while they were at Macclesfield they took the opportunity to have a long day shopping in Manchester. 'We ordered at Holdsworths curtains for Sudeley', Emma recorded. 'For the family dining room crimson cloth with border to match the carving on the panels – a very good idea, I wonder if in years to come anyone will ever notice. In the library we are to have dark plum – with stars. In the upstairs dining room crimson ground with roses and Elizabeth's monogram etc. copied from the cloth which hung behind the celebrated Warwick sideboard in the first Great Exhibition'.

They also went to Thackeray's lecture on George III, which Emma described as 'very sarcastic and clever – and I fear only too true' – and saw the Free Trade Hall lit up by electricity for the first time.

The year 1857 began in Winchcombe with a celebration for the opening of the new school room built by Mr Smith of the Farm. After a service in Winchcombe church, at which the Rev. George Roberts and his choir from Cheltenham sang, Emma and John invited all their neighbours to dine with them, including Mr Bellairs, the Government Inspector of Schools. Then they all went in a body to the school room for a grand tea party to celebrate the beginning of public schools and the public education movement in Winchcombe.

Before that time there were no free schools in the town. John Oakey says he attended the King's School, which had been endowed by Henry VIII from the revenues of Winchcombe Abbey. The master there was Clement Cunningham, and Emma had already had to come to his rescue. 'Cunningham the schoolmaster over head and ears in debt, poor fellow', she wrote 'and hardly to be wondered at considering his little pay. I have 'lent' him, which is equivalent to giving £45 10s to clear him out of his troubles'.

Her own accounts for the school opening included £4 4s 6d to have the Winchcombe organ repaired and tuned for the service, £5 17s 6d to Marshall for lighting the school room for the tea party and £3 15s 0d for bringing the choir out, and for their omnibus expenses.

Although Emma and John were still childless, her brothers' families were growing fast and both Mary and Ann were generous in 'lending' Emma their daughters. Edith, William and Mary's eldest child and Emma's god daughter was a particular favourite and spent months at a time at Sudeley. Marianne wrote to say that William's eldest boy, William, was no longer to be called Bonny but Fitz, which means son of William – and a system of fines had been established to enforce the rule.

Then on 8 June, 1857, Emma wrote 'A sad trial came. In taking a walk to Humblebee with some young friends our dogs attracted the cows, which chased us and so caused a premature confinement by which we lost our hope and child – a very great trial indeed it was'.

This event is something of a mystery. The only information we have on her life up to this point consists of quotes from her own 'pocket books' which she collated and wrote in a family scrap book when she was in her fifties. There is no earlier mention of a pregnancy which, given her great desire for a child, we would have expected to have been noted and announced with great excitement and rejoicing. It may be that it was only after this incident, when presumably she fell and miscarried, that she knew she had been pregnant, and that the damage was severe enough to prevent her, although only 34-years-old at the time, from having any more children.

She does mention consulting the eminent gynaecologist, James Young Simpson, in Edinburgh, much later in her life, in 1864, and she also had an operation in April 1875, which could have been a hysterectomy. The only other clue to this episode is an 'exquisitely embroidered baby's cap, which was embroidered for me when it was rumoured, but alas without foundation that I was going to have a child'. She kept this among her treasures saying, 'there is something very touching about that little cap, which brings tears into my eyes'.

Whatever the truth behind this incident, she had recovered sufficiently by the end of June to go with Marianne, her brothers Peter and Philip and cousin Tom to the opening of the Manchester Exhibition. 'We were in good places and stood close to the crimson carpet down which walked the Queen, Prince Albert, the Princess Royal, the Crown Prince of Russia and the Prince of Wales . . . 'God Save the Queen' was glorious – sung by Simon Reeves and Clara Novelle – a wonderful Exhibition it was of pictures and art treasures, truly'.

Marianne and Emma chose the Lake District for their annual summer holiday that year – beginning with a pilgrimage to Katherine Parr's birthplace, Sizergh Castle, near Kendal and continuing to Ambleside, where Emma had fond memories of a youthful holiday with her Brenchley cousins, who had built and lived in Wanless House. While staying with them then she had visited Wordsworth, who gave her his hand and his blessing, and dined with Coleridge, who promised to write her a sonnet if, after six renditions of 'Give me the Sweetest Flower' she would sing it for him one more time. She obliged with the song, but had since lost the sonnet.

It proved to be an adventurous holiday. 'We took a carriage from Grasmere – but our young driver did not know the road – and with horses tired and hungry began the ascent of Styhead on a road no longer used. Fortunately we were walking to save the poor horses – they began to gib and the carriage went off the road, saved only by a rock from going over a precipice. We were hours before we could gain help – not being able with our united strength – three women and a driver – to pull the carriage back again. Then, our horses being done, we abandoned Styhead and took the road to Ulpha. Again we lost our way and had to plunge thro' a mountain stream – horses again gibbed. I was carried across by the driver, who nearly fell in the middle of the water. How we laughed and how glad we were to find a lodging at night at Ulpha.'

More adventures followed – Marianne climbed Skiddaw and at Keswick Emma found a gallery selling Pettit's pictures. The Pettit family came from Worcester and remembered John's old Uncles as 'young John' and 'young William'. All in all she described it as a 'peaceful, heavenly tour'. Marianne and Emma with faithful Bayliss the maid – driving, posting, lodging for a month – it had cost only £47 6s.

It had been a sad year in Winchcombe. Lane who had worked for 20 years as head carpenter at Sudeley died in October. He had carried out most of the carving and woodwork in the Castle since the start of the restoration work in 1837. Meanwhile smallpox was raging in the town – farmers wives and daughters were afraid to come to town. 'It is dreadful to see little children playing about the streets with the spots in the worst stage for carrying the contagion', Emma noted.

There was drama when John went to London to finalise the purchase of Lord Boston's land adjoining the Castle and was woken by the Vicar Harvey knocking on his bedroom door with the news that Trenfield, the Winchcombe lawyer, 'a great rogue who had been committing forgeries and other iniquities' had been trying to blow his brains out. He recovered but was removed from his office as Clerk to the Magistrates, of whom John was then Chairman, and sentenced to 10 years penal servitude. The Vicar Harvey was also taken to Gloucester Assizes for debt, although Emma had already helped him out once by persuading John to lend him the £40 he owed to his grocer.

Emma said she had kept a note of all her Sunday activities during the year. 'Teaching in Sunday School was my delight – attending school in the morning and having a large class of young women in the afternoon in the upstairs dining room at Sudeley'.

Before the restoration of the Chapel was completed services were held in the small side chapel – 'tall square pews and no singing at all'. Emma then trained her girls to sing the hymns, starting them off in the right key with the aid of a pipe. They sat down the aisle on a very narrow rotten plank which crashed down one sleepy summer afternoon. Fortunately by then a small harmonium had been put into one of the pews and a few months later some of the workmen at the Castle volunteered to form themselves into a choir. Emma took up their offer, but she insisted on some very severe practising and having a master out once a week from Cheltenham to drill and refine them.

She was also busy making plans for an historical party to be held in 1859. Agnes Strickland, the historian came to stay and give advice and brought with her a Mrs Chatson, who in her young days claimed to have danced a minuet with George IV when he was Prince Regent. Emma found Agnes Strickland 'a little vain perhaps and rather pushing in public – but in private tête-à-têtes everything that is agreeable clever and entertaining'. In December Nathan the costumier came to measure them for their historical costumes. Emma noted that her dressmaking bill for the year was £23.

'A princely entertainment on a magnificent scale' was the press description of the Historical Party in January 1959, when Emma and John, in the guise of Henry VIII and Katherine Parr, entertained their guests who had all made great efforts to attend in the appropriate costume of the day. Correct dances of the period were arranged by the Hon F Lygon, 'who sustained the character of Philip II of Spain.'

The hospitality of Sudeley was proverbial in the whole county of Gloucester and, we are told, on this occasion it surpassed itself: a lamb roasted whole graced the bottom of the table; a gigantic woodcock pie the top; two peacocks glittered in their tails and plumage on the side and among the other more conspicuous dishes were a boar's head and a roast cygnet.

Emma, for once, did not report on the occasion, other than to refer to 'many newspaper cuttings'. While it had obviously been a great public success, for her personally, it had not been a happy event, for reasons we shall discover later.

CHAPTER FIVE

'I have often thought that I should like to keep a journal of my everyday life in England, so this bright day in Scarborough I will begin', Emma wrote. 'John is at Gloucester as High Sheriff, attending the Assizes, and I am here with my old friend Mrs Vallance, alias Aunt Kitty (and now nine months a widow) for a fortnight's holiday and rest.'

She seems to have forgotten that she had been keeping a diligent record of her life in various pocket books and journals ever since her marriage in 1847. These, together with family reminiscences from her childhood were written up, laced out with family letters, in a large scrapbook which she compiled, and form the basis of our knowledge of her life to date.

However, now she starts afresh in a 6s 6d leather-bound book bought from S.W. Theakston, booksellers of Scarborough, and this is the beginning of her collected 'Diaries'.

Perhaps it was appropriate that she should have started writing it in Scarborough, which was always one of her favourite places, and already had happy memories for her of times spent there with her brother-in-law Martin, with Marianne and with Susan Wyniatt, a friend from Winchcombe.

'Nothing can surpass to my fancy the beauty of this place', she wrote. 'Our lodgings are charmingly situated facing the sea – giving us a view of the little bay which reminds me constantly of a miniature Naples. The old town to the left with its red roofs and picturesque houses, all sizes, heights and shapes – the castle in ruins towering above the town – the pier, the lighthouse . . . The water is covered with boats and the shores are alive with spectators, for there is a Regatta going on today and all Scarborough is out to see it – boat racing, duck racing and walking on a greased pole for a pig.'

'Last night we were on the bridge till late, listening to the band and watching the promenaders . . . for some time the moon shone out in all her glory, making a golden path on the waters, lighting up the sands and scattering beauty all over the earth and heaven and sea'.

Her fortnight at Scarborough came to an end and she set off home via Hurdsfield, where Uncle William, now in his seventy-sixth year, was dangerously ill. There she learnt that her great uncle Peter Pownall of Bramall had died the year before in his ninety-fourth year – the last of his generation. His faculties were perfect to the end, as were his teeth – a fact he demonstrated by using them to crack some damson stones. According to Emma's father, the old man had been able to see the cows grazing in the field from his bed, and even purchased one that was brought into view, as carefully as ever.

After his death, her brother Philip and cousin Tom discovered a room in his house which had remained unopened for thirty years. When they broke into it with an axe they found the top of the room completely filled with ivy which had crept in through the window – but the contents, which included a spinet, dresses, books, bonnets, gloves, fans and a rouge pot, were all perfectly preserved. They had belonged to his very dear sister Mary and after her death he could not bear to have the room opened.

John did not share Emma's affection for the North-East coast, and after the Assizes finished, instead of joining her at Scarborough, he went to stay with Sam Fielden and his new bride, Sarah Yates. 'They say the match was made at our Historical Party', Emma wrote, 'anyway they were married soon after'. Sarah had caused a sensation at the Party, when she appeared as a Lancashire witch, and stole not only most of the newspaper coverage, but Sam's heart as well. Sam had complained that he was 'bewitched' by Sarah and, as can be imagined, Emma did not care for her much.

The year before he had given Emma his last personal present – a piece of transatlantic cable set as a locket – 'the wires looking like inlaid gold and steel'. From now on they were to seldom meet, and when they did it was usually to try to sort out his sister Ann's problems. 'She has been more an invalid than ever lately' Emma noted, collecting her daughter, Maimie, for a visit to Sudeley while Ann was a patient of Dr. Gully at Malvern.

On arriving back at the Castle she found that Henry had brought their cousin, Julius Brenchley, with him from London. He had been travelling the world for the past ten years, not only visiting all the principal cities in Europe and America, but also spending many months in the court of the King of the Sandwich Islands.

'He is an enormous man and very handsome', Emma reported. Twenty years earlier he had been her first love, but it was his brother Coare who had wanted to marry her and who had recently died, alone and unmarried, claiming never to have recovered from her turning him down. Emma now found Julius 'marvellously improved. Travel and seeing many men of many minds has expanded his soul and improved his expression'. He did not stay long before leaving England again for China and Japan.

Although it was only September, the weather was nearly as cold as Christmas when Emma and John went to the annual Gloucester Music Meeting. Perhaps it was the cold which affected the performers for Emma complained that they sang woefully out of tune and Harper's trumpet 'sounded as if it had a bone in its throat'. She declined to hold a plate at the door after the service, which she was expected to do as the wife of the High Sheriff 'having an objection to publicity which I shall never overcome', she said.

Then came the sad news of the death of Uncle William 'the poor old Squire'. Much to the family's great surprise, he had left Swythamley, the sporting estate in Staffordshire, to Emma's brother Philip, and his Tytherington house and the rest of his property to Emma's father and Uncle Tom, who were to squabble over it for some years to come.

Marianne wrote to Emma: 'Philip left sole undisputed possessor of Swythamley in length and breadth and £7,000 per annum, so goes the Will, made in 1849 after Aunt William's death who, says Uncle William 'extorted' a promise that Pip should have her money and it bought Swythamley. The rest of the property – Tytherington included – is left between Papa and Uncle Tom to be scrambled for – not a scrap to anybody else – pretty for poor William and a pretty bone of contention is Tytherington – Uncle Tom claims it as he says Papa gets Swythamley'.

At Sudeley Emma was glad to be able to start work on planning the garden. The surrounding terraces had been built and on 20 September 1859 she wrote: 'The garden was this morning actually commenced – partly on Nesfield's plan and partly on Mr. Makgill's, the latter I much prefer, the beds etc. being all on the square, whereas Nesfield's is on the round and oval – anyhow the labourers are at work removing the soil, levelling and measuring.' (Emma records paying Nesfield £57 18s for his design – he was one of the leading landscape gardeners at the time).

'The old sheds that had been so long standing between the ruined Banquet Hall and the Dungeon Tower have been taken down, opening the view onto Humble How and improving the whole of the second quadrangle. The ground is to be levelled and made into a bowling green – with beds of flowers and shrubs at the end.'

By November she had a gardener over from Worcester for further advice. 'The beds are now formed and the difficulty is what to do with the two pieces of flat ground between the garden and the terraces. I am most anxious to have an alley on each side, formed of two rows of arches in yew trees, twelve feet high, but Smith says they would cost £170 and therefore the subject will have to be reconsidered.'

We now know that she won her case, for the following April (1860) she reports: 'The last two days there has been great excitement in the garden planting the yew alleys. It is like magic to see the beautiful trees in already – 10ft or 12ft high – furnishing the grounds more than we could possibly have imagined – we must hope they will live and do the garden credit – I can't wait to see them cut into form'. Her total garden bill for 1860 was £200 and as well as the yew hedges this included 480 yards of dwarf box, 800 yards of box and 300 common laurels, fruit trees, vegetables,roses and magnolia.

Inside the Castle she was busy arranging patchwork for the curtains to hang on the old oak bedstead with the Royal Arms which had just been moved into their bedroom, where Emma was determined that 'all the needlework will be my own doing – not quite so elaborate as the work accomplished by the ladies of olden times, but on the whole I feel rather proud of it considering how many other things there are nowadays to interest and occupy us'.

One of these interests was her music. She had inherited a good voice from her mother's musical family, good enough to sing professionally had she had the opportunity. As it was she enjoyed sharing her musical enthusiasm, and decided to start a singing class in Winchcombe, employing Mr Bliss, the musical tutor from Cheltenham training college to teach the schoolchildren and train the Chapel choir.

Then she began a small Glee Club among her friends. 'At our first meeting we mustered very well', she wrote. '2 Miss Hollands, Mr Wyniatt and two of his sisters, Mr and Mrs Leigh, who have lately come to reside at Lord Ellenborough's house at Prescott, Mr Pruen of Didbrook and Mr Makgill and his daughter. We tried chiefly Mendelssohn's four part songs. The evening passed very pleasantly and I think we may have made a good beginning'.

On the social scene she and John were invited for the first time to dine at Toddington. Emma was not impressed with Lord Sudeley. 'Lord S took me into dinner and very much he puzzled me in his style of conversation', Emma wrote, 'pretending to know nothing, referring to Mr Holland constantly for confirmation of all he said – and if he is what he pretends to be, he is one of the most empty-headed, bloated aristocrats I have the pleasure of knowing'. Lady Sudeley on the other hand she found to be a gentle, kind, good little woman and their eldest daughter Julia particularly amiable. 'We had a gorgeous dinner and half a dozen powdered flunkies to wait upon us,'she recalled.

The Dents had a procession of visitors at Sudeley. First Emma's eldest brother, William came to stay with Mary and their three children, Edith, Fitz and Arthur. 'There being no nursery here it required a little scheming where to lodge them most comfortably', Emma wrote. 'They were all very good and seemed extremely happy, the boys in particular in going up to see the keepers on the hill to see the dogs and ferrets.'

They were followed by Emma's second cousins, the

Ramsbottoms. 'We took them on some dirty country walks, which gave us all a great deal of amusement, particularly as they, living at Dover, are not much accustomed to walk beyond the promenades, and we had great difficulty and fun in getting them over the stiles and thro' the muddy lanes'.

Finally there was a return visit from cousin Julius Brenchley, who continued to amaze them with the strange habits and tastes he had acquired. 'At breakfast, for example, he eats an enormous amount of beef steak and drinks a bottle of champagne – a whole bottle – and instead of being the worse is all the better for it. He says he really prefers raw fish to cooked and has constantly eaten game uncooked – once among the savages he was forced to eat a piece of human flesh'. Despite, or perhaps because of all this at the age of forty-six 'he has not a grey hair, his limbs are as strong as iron, his skin as fine as possible'.

It was to be their first Christmas at Sudeley and they were on their own except for Marianne. On Christmas Eve Emma's Fife and Drum Band came up to the Castle and played all their best and most military tunes, and then the '18 Fifers, 4 Drums and 2 Triangles were refreshed with as much roast beef and plum pudding as they could eat.' Emma always enjoyed dressing up, and for the servants party on Boxing Day she and Marianne appeared on the balcony of the servants hall, Marianne in the Bear's Dress and Emma as Old Christmas and lowered Christmas presents to all the servants and their families.

Marianne was still with them in the New Year when, following a spate of balls, Emma wrote 'we have been quite dissipated for us'. All eyes were on Henry Coventry, the nephew of the Hon Tom Coventry, who had been their landlord at Severn Bank, who was paying marked attention to Marianne. At the end of January he proposed and, much to Emma's delight, they became engaged. She thoroughly approved of Henry and as he now lived at Woolstone, only five miles from Sudeley, she was excited at the prospect that Marianne might settle near them.

However, there was still the hurdle of John Brocklehurst's consent and she and Marianne waited anxiously for his response to the news of the match. 'We wrote to him the day before yesterday and yet no answer', Emma complained. 'If he had sent us one short note we should have thought it so kind – but men don't think of these things'.

The answer when it came was a resounding no. 'My father won't hear of it – nothing we can say has any effect', Emma wrote. 'He is perfectly hard and obdurate, has wounded my feelings more deeply than ever they were wounded before. He refused to see Henry Coventry at all. Marianne I cannot understand. All I feel is that a beautiful future is clouded, a mirror broken never to be joined; and I fear I feel we shall never be again what we have been to one another – never quite the same.' Emma seemed to have forgotten that she had been subjected to, and caved in under similar pressure, over her own proposed engagement to Robert Chester, and because she was so in favour of Henry Coventry she now took her father's objections to him almost personally.

As it was Marianne went to see her father in London and then went home to Hurdsfield, leaving

Emma to pick up the pieces. 'I saw Henry Coventry a few days ago and I was obliged to tell him my father's objections were not only on the score of want of property, but that the Coventry family generally were not such as he would have his daughter marry into – even the present young Earl is already so much on the Turf'.

'It was a very sad interview, but I believe we both felt better for it and at the end of three hours conversation we came to the conclusion we could not ever be so utterly wretched again. That now there was nothing to be done but wait and see if my father would relent after a time. But still Henry is so full of hope and trust that it wrings my heart to think what I believe, that there is still the bitterest disappointment in store for him,' she said.

Emma was right. John Brocklehurst never did relent and Marianne was not prepared to stand out against him and marry the man she loved, even with Emma's support, Henry and Emma always remained friends and some eight years later – in 1868 – he married Leila Craven.

Meanwhile Emma herself was suffering from her recurrent disenchantment with her own life. 'I often wonder if others suffer from the overwhelming feeling I have that my life is passing away so rapidly and I accomplish nothing – that my days are actually frittered away – however well I may contemplate occupying my time still when evening comes, there has been nothing done. I wish I could think of some great good deed to do, or learn to look at the little events of the hour as being in themselves worthy of my time and thought'.

She started some literary endeavours. The publishers, John Murray were about to publish a *Handbook on Gloucestershire*, and through John's great friend William Cooke, who was a connection of John Murray's, Emma had been asked to check the information referring to Sudeley and its neighbourhood. There were also discussions going on about starting an *Amateur Magazine* – Mr Aspinall Dudley, the Chaplain of Gloucester Jail, had agreed to be the editor and several of Emma's friends had promised to write articles for a publication which they laughingly suggested could compete with, or even threaten, Thackeray's *Cornhill Magazine*.

Another of her interests was the gyroscope – then a new invention by a Frenchman, which aimed to prove that inertia is a property of matter in motion as well as of matter at rest; that orbital and axial motions are connected and may resemble each other. 'A beautiful scientific plaything', she said.

Emma and John had planned a trip to Europe that summer and she was not very pleased at his insistence that Marianne should go with them; 'I tried to behave as if I was enjoying myself – I am certain I enjoyed the landing, the pottage and the feeling we were once more on foreign soil.'

Her diary then erupts into capitals with the announcement 'I HAVE SEEN THE EMPEROR! the greatest man of his age. He was in an open carriage with the Empress – driving in the Bois de Boulogne. At first he was looking in the opposite direction, the Empress seeing our interest directed his attention to us – his countenance lighted up in a moment, his eagle like eyes were directed towards us and he smiled and raised his hat.'

A few days later she was to see him again, when an amateur photographer friend of her cousin's husband M. Traitt, was expecting the Royal family at his house in Paris for a photographic session. Forewarned of this, they had a good vantage point and were able to watch the Emperor lift the young prince out of the carriage, while the Empress followed without her bonnet.

They left Paris *sans regrets* and determined not to visit the French Opera again which had proved 'long, tedious and badly acted – though the Dress Circle fairly sparkled with diamonds' – and set off on their journey through France – by steamer from Bayonne to St Sebastian in Spain and then adventurously by carriage through the Pyrenees. But the bitter disappointment which Emma still felt over the failure of all her hopes for Marianne and Henry Coventry still lingered and clouded everything. 'I intended to write down so many thoughts and feelings tonight' she wrote in a town astride a torrent in the Pyrenees 'but I am so sad I can only record my sorrow.'

And again in Geneva, comparing the scenery to her last visit she commented 'the lakes and mountains are unchanged – only if possible more beautiful than ever. Why do these mountains, lakes and forests never disappoint us and our fellow creatures ever?'

The return to Sudeley was no happier. 'A great deal has been done – the roof put on the little side chapel – balustrade up between the yew hedge and the stables – and most of the rest ready to put up. The old place looked very interesting and I thought we had not seen anything more so in our travels, but at present, owing to disappointments and coldness I seem under a cloud'.

She decided to give up the idea of the *Amateur Magazine* which appeared to be a bone of contention between her and John, and promised not to take on any new schemes for the present.

A few evenings later 'John was coming to read me Ruskin's last volume when I very unnecessarily found fault with him for playing with and spoiling a paper cutter I intended for a prize. He became impatient – words followed – he left the room – but returned in a few minutes saying when his evil spirit mastered him he was ready to resent anything I said impatiently, but when his better spirit prevailed he remembered how very often he had been unkind to me when unprovoked and he would try to take all I might ever say quietly and patiently. The chapter he was going to read in Ruskin's book was on "Peace"', Emma recalled.

It was a wet and miserable Autumn. John had gout, and Emma was banished to sleep in a small iron bedstead in the dressing room. 16 September was their thirteenth wedding anniversary. 'It rained then, it rains now', she wrote. She was reading the *Recreations of a Country Parson* which commended the keeping of a diary, recording how the hours were spent.

'What a splendid diary mine would be', she exclaimed. 'Waiting on the invalid and studying Spanish till half past eleven. Stitch, stitch at the 6th Angel for the altar cloth until 2 o'clock dinner time – more Spanish – inclined to headache – went out – called at the redbrick cottage – talked to the eldest girl, got her to promise to be industrious, to clear up before her mother came home from reaping, then walked to Humblebee Cottage – paid Alice Bolton a long visit – promised her 6 yds of flannel and odds and ends for filling pillows – called also next door – admired the baby, increased cleanliness etc., – then on to the tenants of Wadfield Farm – looked at their alterations in kitchen and passages, chatted a few minutes with the stonemasons and so home – prepared patchwork for schoolchildren – headache so much worse, went to bed early. Call that work? How much is said and written about work nowadays. I wish someone would write a book and define work and give women in circumstances as I am more difficult work to do'.

She turned her attention to Winchcombe and met with the ladies of the town to divide it into districts for visiting. Emma's share was the lane between the two turnpikes – all the houses at the foot of White Hart Hill and the right hand side of Silk Mill Lane. The next Sunday she began visiting them – 'read prayers and scripture to poor old Troughton and had a long talk with Mrs Butcher, who took the pledge more than a year ago and has kept it. I lent her to read *Haste to the Rescue* and she seemed very pleased at my having called upon her and spoken encouragingly.'

Night Schools were started in the town, and even John became interested enough to teach a class of girls one evening. His interest faltered, but Emma continued to teach classes, as often as twice a week, trudging across the fields accompanied by a boy with a lantern to stop her stumbling over the sleeping cows. In February 1861 there was a 'hurricane', which destroyed part of Gloucester station and left Cheltenham a scene of devastation, tiles and chimney pots flung about in all directions. As Emma walked to the Night School that evening 'the wind carried me over the fields with a run, returning I came by the road, and never heard so fearful a howling as the wind made amongst the trees. I ran by them fearful they might fall on me – and indeed it was very dangerous, two or three fell after I passed, but there was something in the wild scene that I enjoyed extremely.'

As well as her activities in Winchcombe Emma was keen to start a school in Gretton, and was busy organising fund-raising ventures for this project. A sale of work raised £15 and an Amateur Concert £37 11s from the sale of tickets. She also began 'wood sawing' (known later as fretwork) and, to her great surprise, succeeded in making a small book stand 'with only breaking two saws, but they are very fine – 6d a dozen and the frame cost 7s 6d. This became her new hobby, and as she had now finished sewing the altar cloth for the chapel 'sawing' replaced 'stitching' in the everyday accounts in her diary.

All this time work had been continuing on the restoration of the Chapel. Gilbert Scott was now in great demand for church restorations both in England and on the Continent, so although he kept overall control of the work at Sudeley his assistant architect J. Drayton Wyatt was left in charge, perhaps fortuitously for Sudeley, as he was to become a very good friend to the Dents and to Winchcombe.

John was determined that the substantial legacy which Uncle John Dent had left for the restoration of the Chapel should be well spent and that the building should be a fitting memorial both for Katherine Parr and for the Dent uncles. Rattee & Kett of Cambridge undertook all the wood and stone carving and Frederick Preedy of Worcester designed and made the stained glass windows, with suggestions for the subjects from John and Emma. J. Birnie Philip, who was later to become known for his work on the Albert Memorial in Hyde Park, was employed to carve Katherine Parr's tomb and the Chapel reredos.

In April 1861 Katherine Parr's leaden coffin was moved for the last time and her remains 'a little brown dust' put into the new tomb, and the old cracked chapel bell given by 'Lady Dorotie Chandos widdowe' which had been recast was rehung.

CHAPTER SIX

Travelling was always Emma's greatest pleasure and one of the few enthusiasms which she and John shared, and it seems likely that he was responsible for making their travel plans and itineraries. Although travel in the nineteenth century was comparatively cheap, it was far from comfortable. The railways had to a large extent replaced the diligence as the means of travel between major towns, but for anything more adventurous it was often necessary to hire a carriage, as they had done in the Pyrenees, or to travel by post carriage as they were now planning – first to cross the Col du Mont Cenis into Italy, and then return over the St Gothard Pass.

Emma was in a philosophical mood as they set off: 'On the 25th, in the sunshine, as the clock struck midday – John and I and Bayliss the maid started on our travels. It seemed a few days ago as if it would be impossible to bring one's little worldly affairs to a close and make arrangements for leaving home. But by dint of hard work and late hours the last arrangement was at last made, the final order given and as we rolled away I thought how soon, in five minutes perhaps, the domestic workers would cease to regret us – and I could not help thinking how like it all is to life and death. We fancy the world will stand still without us, our little world at least, and all our little plans will come to naught when we are gone – but is it so? The time for our long journey thro' the Dark Valley comes – we hurry our arrangements – we leave injunctions to some – loving remembrances to a few (how few when there are so many to love) – and at our departure others with fresher spirits take up our work. Ere the passing bell has ceased to toll, the keen regret is over and we are hardly remembered. Oh how with such thoughts as these can any of us be proud?'

Perhaps it was the same feeling of destiny and past memories which made John decide to visit Windsor and Eton before they left England and revisit the haunts of his schooldays. Now he showed Emma where lessons were learnt, games played and fights fought, although he was disappointed to find that no-one at Eton now recognised him, not even Old Spanky the general sweetware man who said 'Lor sir how you are altered'.

They journeyed through France and reached Turin to find the city celebrating its status as the new capital of a free and unified Italy. (In 1859 Cavour, premier of Sardinia, with the support of Napoleon III had driven the Austrians from Lombardy – in 1860 Garibaldi and his 'thousand red shirts' took Sicily and in 1861 Victor Emmanuel, King of Sardinia, became King of all Italy, except Venetia and Rome). Following their honeymoon experiences in

1848 Emma and John seemed destined to be in Italy during such momentous events.

Amid all the rejoicing, Cavour, who had been the architect of Italian unification, died while they were in Turin. 'It is said the Dr bled him too profusely for apoplexy, but as it was his fourth attack and 52 years of age everything was against him'. Emma reported. 'The principal shops are closed – crowds have assembled at his house – on the pillars of the door are black cloths and the bulletin of his death'.

They travelled back over the St Gothard Pass, involving four changes of horses, into Switzerland and Bavaria, staying in small country hotels – often *au troisieme* – which presumably meant three to a room, with Bayliss the maid.

It was very hot – ninety degrees in the hotel room – when they reached Munich with its 500 Beer houses. 'Everyone drinks and talks of beer – the artist mixes his colours in beer – the dullest become enthusiastic on the subject of beer', Emma wrote. 'Munich has a name for being a very dissolute city, but there is some sort of law which prevents people marrying unless they have a certain sum to live upon, the consequence is half the population is illegitimate'. The present King was described as very amiable but not overdone with brains. His father, Ludwig I, who had been a civilising influence on the city, had been forced to abdicate following unrest over his relationship with the dancer Lola Montez.

When they returned to Sudeley there was the usual procession of visitors, even though Emma said she and John were never so happy as when they were quite alone. 'How difficult it is with guests in the house to get thro' any work', she complained. 'I leave mine for an hour or two after breakfast and greatly enjoy the quiet and repose of the little crimson room. Today, while all were playing billiards I made my escape and wrote and read and practised Hopkins *Te Deum* till luncheon'.

Education was the main subject of the day. The Government was concerned that the money it gave to the elementary schools was not being well spent, and was trying to devise a new scheme for examining both pupils and schools. Emma had at last raised enough money to start a small school in Gretton and William's children, Edith, Fitz and Arthur were all at school in Cheltenham.

The first services were being held in the Chapel, although it had not been re-dedicated yet, and John had been to consult the Bishop about providing a curate for the new parish – the Dents having agreed to pay the principal part of his stipend.

Emma still regretted the restoration. 'It seems such a short time since it was open to the sky – since the floor was covered with soft greensward and the walls hung with ivy and roses. It was then truly an historical record of an eventful period in our history – now it seems a mental effort to grasp the past and appreciate the building with anything save modern, though beautiful windows and marble floors. Scott, Philip and Preedy have done their best – and already their names seem more associated with it than Cromwell and his ruthless soldiers – pleased as I am that the Chapel has been so exquisitely restored and that it was perhaps our duty not to leave the House of God in ruins, still I cannot help regretting deeply and

Emma with Busy

<u>May Day</u> – a snow storm in the morning & in the afternoon –

I have written to the Duke of Bedford to thank him for his very interesting catalogue of the Woburn Abbey pictures – Several of the Chandoses are named therein – and their portraits well described –

M[r] Prosser the Mayor of Tewkesbury has sent me a drawing of the chain (Badge) presented to him by M[r] Price, M.P. I have suggested to him to have his portrait taken wearing the official chain & to present it to the Town

<u>2nd</u> I wrote ten letters & notes – In the aft[n] called at Infants' Sch – Miss Freeman explained her disappointment that 17 of her children did not pass at the Examination because the Insp[r] puzzled them in the Tables – asking them 6 eights? instead of 6 times 8? at Dents Sch: I listened to lessons given – at Jacobite House, saw how the pump had been removed to the back from the street corner. Curtains put up in sitting room of my workn – little trees growing well – tiles put round garden – In Alms Houses I saw 5 of the inmates who all thanked me for having the bells put up in their bed-rooms –

3rd Long conversation with housekeeper Bayliss – who told me many discouraging things of the ingratitude of Winchcombe people – I said how I had loved, prayed for, worked for & devoted myself to Winchcombe – & I did not think there was any love in return – she said when Prince Albert was alive, no one thought any thing of him – now he was dead, enough c[oul]d not be said in his praise! I thought it a very pretty way to put it –

18th Avenue of Beeches planted! they will grow up
and cast their pretty shadows, and spread out their
arms to catch the rays of sun - and men & women
will walk by them, children will play under them, but

Dec - 1891

there will be no one to remember the old lady who
lovingly planted them, always in memory of those who are
gone!
23rd came Marianne, Miss Booth, Miss Ryan —

Christmas day, everything white with hoar frost
Influenza raging everywhere - servants had it in
turns - but mildly —

During the year I have walked more than 1134 miles.

I have had to Breakfast 500.
       - Luncheon - 604
       Dinner - 596
       Tea - 1491
          ——
         2191

Emma's tutor, Senor Bruno

The MBs – Marianne Brocklehurst (above) and Mary Booth

Emma's husband, John Coucher Dent

Emma, photographed by Silvy in 1866

Sunday afternoon on the lake at Zurich – 'a great deal of fear and
very little danger!'

The Channel Crossing – Boulogne to Folkestone – Emma was a poor sailor

An 'adventure' with Marianne in the Lake District

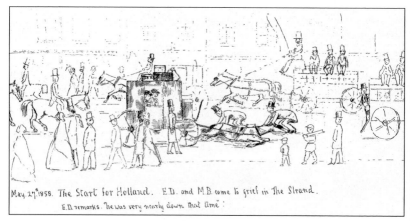

An accident in The Strand

Emma feeding her white pigeons, with Mr Haines and Busy the dog

Milkmaids at Sudeley, 1864

Emma in her drawing room at Sudeley

A shooting party, 1893

Gardners with 'the old rattling mowing machine', 1857

The Jubilee Fountain in
the Queen's Garden at
Sudeley, 1897

The Jubilee Fair at Sudeley, 1897

Skating on the lake, 1884

Building the bonfire on Langley Hill for Queen Victoria's Golden Jubilee, 1887

Building the North Tower, 1890

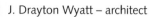
J. Drayton Wyatt – architect

The North Tower completed

Page from the *Winchester and Sudeley Record* – the local magazine Emma published in Winchcombe

The Winchcombe and Sudeley Record.

Vol. 35; No. 3.   **NOVEMBER, 1892.**   HALF-PENNY.

Witchcraft, Funerals, &c.—continued.

IN a small collection at Sudeley Castle, of Roman curiosities, perhaps the most curious are some little flattened drops of iridescent glass, presented to me many years ago by Signor Fiorelli, the distinguished custodian of the Neapolitan Museum. At the same time he explained how very much they had puzzled Italian Archæologists, who, after much consideration, came to the conclusion that as they were always *found in tombs*, these little dabs or drops of glass represented expiatory or propitiatory *tears* for the dead.

Both here and in many other places there is a superstition against burying a woman with even her wedding ring on. A story is told of a gentleman who wished when his mother died, that her wedding ring should be left on her hand, but those who laid her out said: "Ye mun no send her to God wi' her trinkets about her." This, however, may have originated with the Romans, who had a law, B.C., 449, forbidding gold being buried with the dead, except such as had been used for the fastening of teeth.*

Another exceedingly strange funeral custom which was practised in Herefordshire 200 years ago, was that of giving to some poor person, a loaf, and a bowl of beer (which he was to drink up), and sixpence in money, by which means he was supposed to carry off all the sins of the deceased. The man was called the sin eater. † The cake, loaf, and beer given to him was possibly the origin of cakes and wine being afterwards supplied to mourners and guests at funerals.

This reminds us of another superstitious custom still found here, and in other remote districts, of charming away witches by putting into bottles parings of nails, and cuttings of hair, and burying them in consecrated ground.

From the Saxon "Leechdoms," edited by the late Rev. O. Cockayne, it would appear that the burying of charms in "wall-roots" was familiar even to our Saxon forefathers, who also made drinks for fiend-sick men, to be *drunk out of church bells*. The use of holy water, holy oil, and so forth, to expel demons, is also very ancient. The idea of the sacredness of wedding rings, of churchyards, &c., continued to a later period, and in the 17th century became mixed up with the belief in "*sympathy*," "transplantation," and the like. Later still, the idea of a sacred place being necessary for the burial of these antidotes was lost; and it was sufficient if it were a healthy one (not likely to be disturbed by one's enemies), in which the weakness of the afflicted party might quietly be buried and thus got rid of for ever. §

* Leisure Hour.   † See Elton's "Origin of English History"; p. 181.
§ Archæologia, Society of Antiquaries, London ; v. 40., p. 133.

First Glos'ter Volunteers Royal Engineers.

Regimental Camp, Winchcombe.

ATHLETIC SPORTS,

ON

FRIDAY AFTERNOON, JUNE 13,

AT 2-30,

Under the patronage of Lieut.-Colonel Rogers,
Commandant.

1. WHEELBARROW RACE   ...   .   Four Men per Company.
2. THROWING CRICKET BALL   ...   ...   One Man per Company.
3. QUARTER MILE RACE   ...   .   One Man per Company.
4. PICKABACK RACE   ...   .   Four Men per Company.
5. HURDLE RACE ...   .   Two Men per Company.
6. BUCKET RACE   ...   .   Two Men per Company.
7. STEEPLECHASE (from point to point) 1st, 2nd, and 3rd prizes,
   For Members of Battalion.
   DITTO   ...   1st, 2nd, and 3rd prizes, for STRANGERS.
8. MILE RACE ...   .   One Man per Company.
9. THREE-LEGGED RACE   ...   .   Four Men per Company.
10. TUG OF WAR   ...   .   Six Men per Company.
11. DITTO ...   .   Officers v. Winning Team.
12. HURDLE RACE   ...   .   One Man per Company.
13. SACK RACE ...   .
14. VETERAN'S RACE (Handicap) ... One yard per year of Service.
15. HALF-MILE RACE   ...   .   One Man per Company.

*A number of valuable Prizes have been generously
given by Mrs. DENT, of Sudeley Castle.*

Admission to the Abbey Grounds, Threepence.
Holders of Weekly Tickets admitted free.

Entries to be notified to the COMPANY SERGEANT-MAJORS.

Belcher, Printer, North Street, Winchcombe.

Programme for the Sports Day held at the Regimental Camp, Winchcombe

Planting a maze by 'The Grange' (the Tithe Barn)

A dinner for the 1st Gloucester Volunteers Royal Engineers in the Long Room

Portrait of Emma Dent by Josiah Rushton

Emma Dent's ticket to attend Queen Victoria's Coronation, 1838

The chapel and Sudeley Castle from the north east before restoration

Sudeley Chapel – now St Mary's Church – after its restoration by Sir George Gilbert Scott

William Dent

John Dent

By diligence to Barcelona – the two drivers started racing

William Dent starting as High Sheriff in 1851 to meet the Judges at Overbridge – Uncles John and Benjamin Dent and John Coucher Dent are standing in the doorway. Painting by Charles Cattermole

Emma Dent dressed as Katherine Parr for the Historical Party in 1859

John Coucher Dent dressed as Henry VIII for the Historical Party in 1859

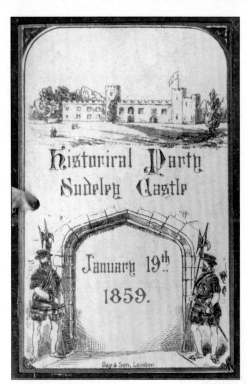

Dance Programmes for the Historical Party, 1859

Historical Party
Sudeley Castle

January 19th
1859.

Day & Son, London

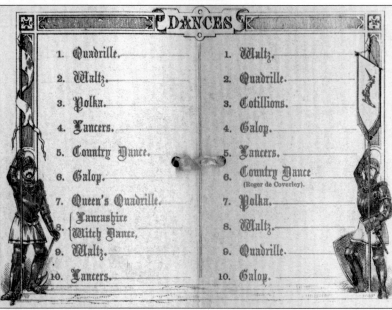

DANCES

1.	Quadrille.	1.	Waltz.
2.	Waltz.	2.	Quadrille.
3.	Polka.	3.	Cotillions.
4.	Lancers.	4.	Galop.
5.	Country Dance.	5.	Lancers.
6.	Galop.	6.	Country Dance (Roger de Coverley).
7.	Queen's Quadrille.	7.	Polka.
8.	Lancashire Witch Dance.	8.	Waltz.
9.	Waltz.	9.	Quadrille.
10.	Lancers.	10.	Galop.

New Year's greeting cards in
1884

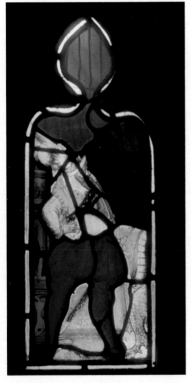

Stained glass window in the restored
chapel

Katherine Parr's tomb in the restored chapel – designed by Sir George Gilbert Scott and carved by J. Birnie Phillip

The yew alleys which Emma planted in 1860 still 'furnish' the gardens at Sudeley

sincerely that the historical record must of necessity be quickly obliterated'.

She was disappointed also that they had just lost the chance of buying one of Katherine Parr's letters. It had been sold at Puttock & Simpsons for £27 10s having only raised £13 ten years earlier. Emma had persuaded John to write up to London and ask Mr Cooke to bid up to £25 for it 'but a private gentleman from the country had given a commission to buy it at any cost – so we lost it'.

The Dents were busy preparing for a Christmas Fancy Ball at Sudeley when the news came on 14 December 1861 of the death of Prince Albert, and they decided to postpone the event for a month out of respect. 'The Queen only just recovering from the loss of her Mother and this great calamity has fallen on her – Prince Albert only 42', Emma wrote.

She did, however, go ahead with another of her Amateur Concerts, performing first at Stanton and then at Winchcombe, where 140 people were assembled in the National School Room. 'Everyone was so kind and encored me as if they really liked my songs and one of the farmers said to John he "liked to hear her sing, her turned it out so easy".' Emma herself admitted that she enjoyed singing in public more than in society, and although she felt at forty she was getting too old to sing she was enjoying it more now than ever.

The Fancy Ball, which was postponed until January, was quite a small event for them – only 100 guests – which meant they could accommodate them in the Castle without having to hire marquees. The dining room became the gentlemen's robing room, the library for the ladies – billiard room for tea – Chandos for reception – Oriel for dancing and the upstairs dining room for supper. Emma went as Gammer Gretel and John as an Old English Gentleman. 'We had tableaux vivants and songs and it was kept up until six o'clock (the next morning) and all said it was a very merry evening'.

They had been planning a tour of Spain for some time, which was one of the reasons why Emma had been teaching herself Spanish, but she was dismayed when once again John invited Marianne to go with them. 'I don't know why but I am sorry – perhaps because we were happier than usual last trip when we went alone . . . I do not enter into this with the slightest pleasurable anticipation,'.

They travelled by train to Perpignan and then set off for Barcelona – John, Emma and Marianne in the coupe and Bayliss in a 'coin' in the interior of the diligence – five changes of horses and twenty-one hours of travel before them. Emma was horrified when a second diligence appeared on the road alongside them and the two drivers started racing. 'At one moment our wheels were within a few inches of each other – there was no way of getting at the driver or conductor except by seizing the lash end of the whip, which when not used in the race just touched my window. – I seized it frantically and so down clambered the conductor to assure Madame, who was looking more dead than alive, that they would keep *en arrière*. What a relief it was to arrive in Barcelona and go to bed for 24 hours.'

Spain was full of discomforts and surprises – like the fleas in Valencia. 'MB and I literally devoured', until Emma sent for some garlic, which when liberally rubbed over the pillow and bed seemed to keep them away. Just as beer had been the prevailing influence in Bavaria, in Spain it was the bullring. The Valencians were reputed to be the most bloodthirsty of the Spanish: 'the poorest would deprive themselves of food and sell their beds to go to the bullfights'.

They went to their first bullfight in Seville – 'that wonderful arena full of 10,000 spectators'. As would be expected Emma did not enjoy the spectacle – 'the most atrocious, inhuman, sanguinary sight I ever witnessed or could possibly have imagined – I shall never forget the relief I felt to get out of that sanguinary place and breathe again fresh air. Returning to the hotel it was most soothing to listen to the band of music in the 'cortile' filled with flowers and shrubs, and a doctrinal discussion with the priest helped to bring in more civilised thoughts when John returned full of descriptions of more horrors and marvellous feats by Tato (the matador)'.

The priest she referred to was a tall, soft-footed young man from Gibraltar, who was on his way to England and was as anxious to practice his English as she was her Spanish. 'Rather curious to find myself in theological dispute with a Spanish priest six feet high – but we always end up by paying ourselves the compliment of saying we believe the other will go to Heaven', she said.

An old school friend of John's – Colonel Hinde – was stationed in Gibraltar and they sailed there next, having visited Duff Gordon & Company's sherry vaults in Jerez on the way. Unexpectedly they bumped into Emma's cousin, Charlie Brocklehurst of The Fence, who was in Gibraltar to meet his brother Frank on his return from a tour round the world. All the Brocklehursts were enthusiastic and intrepid travellers.

Although Emma enjoyed their three months in Spain she found it was a relief to return to the comfort of the London Coffee House after the Spanish *fondas*. She accompanied Sam Fielden to the Handel Festival at the Crystal Palace and decided that she was more in love than ever with her own countrymen and women, and that in all her wanderings she had seen nothing more interesting than the Crystal Palace, heard nothing to compare to the Festival and seen no view more admirable, rich and soft than the view from the terraces.

The only problems were at Stanhope Gate, Henry's London house, where he and Ann were now living on wretched terms. Sam had persuaded them to shake hands and promise to make a fresh start, but Ann said she feared she was incapable of making Henry happy or of doing all she ought to do as wife and mother.

There were several more visits to London that year, to see the great International Exhibition – 'a collection of all that is most interesting from all the corners of the globe – united and classified under one roof'. This marked the beginning of Emma's own passion for collecting. She tried to buy some of the exhibits for a museum which she hoped to form at Sudeley, but found that nearly everything had already been promised to other museums, although she bought 'out of China a bird's nest (from which they make soup) a cash sabre and a few other curiosities.'

The discovery of some foreign coins at Speilmann, the moneychanger in the City, decided her to start a collection of current coins,and this was boosted by Heaton of the Birmingham mint who sent her paper impressions of some of the coins being made there for countries like Venezuela, Siam and Persia.

Autograph collecting then was all the rage and when her young protégé Bessie Calrow gave her Garibaldi's autograph, Emma began what was to become a very extensive and distinguished collection of autographs – including the Duke of Wellington, Paganini, Charles Darwin, Edward Jenner and all the leading politicians, authors, poets and artists of the day.

At first she had dismissed stamps as being of no interest, having 'neither the pleasure of association nor beauty', but she was soon collecting these too, particularly when she began to receive interesting specimens from Brocklehurst relatives and other friends scattered around the world. While on a visit to Paris, she had been amazed to find that stamp swapping among French children had reached such a pitch that the Tuileries Gardens had become known as 'La Petite Bourse' and the police had had to forbid their use for buying and selling stamps.

In the nineteenth century the Cotswold hills, which had been grazed by sheep since Saxon times, were turned by the plough for the first time, and interesting discoveries made beneath the surface. At Sudeley in April 1863 a ploughman working in a field on the Wadfield Farm struck a stone and further digging in the area led to the discovery of the near perfect ruins of a Roman villa. Emma was very excited by the find, particularly as it included part of a tessellated pavement in near perfect condition. Unfortunately news of the discovery soon spread around Winchcombe, and when she found that people were taking pieces of the pavement for souvenirs she hastily made arrangements for it to be moved. John Oakey remembers taking up a portion of the floor in half inch squares forming the figure of the Emperor Constantine and other figures, and relaying it in one of the greenhouses at the Castle. Emma spent the next few weeks on her knees working on its restoration. It was to be the start of many more excavations and discoveries of Roman remains to be found on the Sudeley estate.

With no children of her own, Emma still longed to be able to share her culture and enthusiasms with young people. Bessie Calrow was the daughter of one of Emma's oldest friends and when she left Cheltenham Ladies College spent several years at Sudeley learning 'to cultivate good habits in the spending of time'. Although Bessie was not artistic, she was encouraged by Emma to read Ruskin and Mrs Jameson and to familiarise herself with the paintings of the great masters, and this was to stand her in good stead when Emma and John invited her to accompany them on their next extended European tour.

This time they dawdled through France and Italy – spent time in Florence and Rome, where Emma took the opportunity to have a lesson in mosaic working – and visited the excavations at Pompeii. Finally Emma conquered her aversion to the sea sufficiently to undertake a five day voyage to

Constantinople and she was immediately fascinated by the city. 'It is a wonderful relief to be where there are no galleries of paintings or churches to be visited. The pictures are all outside and the churches are not open to us,' she said.

One day they crossed in a caique to Scutari – landing in Asia for the first time – and walked to see the Howling Dervishes performing their strange dancing rituals at their convent, before crossing the plain where the English tents had been pitched during the Crimean War to find the English burial ground and Montagu Bell's grave. Emma bought some daisy plants there to give to his mother, and collected some other flowers which she planned to dry and send to Florence Nightingale.

As they journeyed back from Constantinople, across the Bosphoros and up the Danube to Budapest, Vienna and Salzburg, Emma became nostalgic for her youth and earlier journeys there with the Osbornes and Henry. 'How madly I enjoyed everything then – since then how subdued I have become and what changes we have all seen. Mrs Osborne died after being separated from her husband, and the world, said after living a very intemperate life. Mr Osborne with a second wife and two little children living at Rossall (where he was headmaster) is oh so changed and broken down. Henry now the father of six children, and if he and his wife are to be believed they lead anything but a happy life'.

How different the travel arrangements were also – then it had taken two days and nearly two nights travelling by diligence from Boulogne to Paris – now the same journey by express train only took 5½ hours, but apart from the night work, she still preferred the 'old way' to the uninteresting train travel, when there was nothing to be seen from the time they got in to the time they got out.

The bells of Winchcombe were rung as a welcome home for their return to Sudeley, and ten years after his Uncle's death, John finally untangled the legal problems which had affected his legacies to Winchcombe so that work could begin on the Dent Almshouses and Dents School.

The Almshouses were built on the site of the Bell Inn and were designed by George Gilbert Scott and built by John Oakey. All the oak used in the buildings came from the Sudeley estate and John Dent reckoned that they cost him £2,000 above the £2,000 legacy. The first occupants were all elderly retainers from the Dents household, who enjoyed talking of the old Uncles and John and his brother Martin when they were boys and 'used to get their feet wet'. Mrs Hill, who had been the Uncles' cook and housekeeper in Worcester, had a beautiful white cockatoo which Martin had brought her from Australia.

For some years the Dents had been trying to solve the school situation by using Uncle John's legacy to buy the National School from Mr Smith of the Farm. When this finally proved impossible John bought Beech Cottage, next to Winchcombe church for 500 guineas and it was agreed that in future the school would be divided with 130 of the older children being taught in the Dents School and the infants remaining in Mr Smith's schoolroom.

On 1 January 1868 the children assembled for the last time in Mr Smith's old room and came to the new school where there was a dinner of roast beef and plum pudding prepared for them, and in the evening ninety mothers were invited to tea. As John was away, Emma decided it was up to her to say a few words for the occasion, and after thanking Mr Smith she said;

'I hope you really feel that we are all very anxious to help you in educating your children – I say in helping because the great principal part of education you know must be done in your own homes by your own firesides – I often feel a very great responsibility in living in the big castle and having so many more of the good things of this life than you, and when I hear the voice of God telling me to help my sisters, it always seems as if they are most to be helped by helping their children –'

'You can help us again to do this by sending them punctually, clean and neat – encouraging them to tell you of what they are learning, taking an interest in their different lessons. Miss Malins desires me to tell you that the bell will ring at five minutes to nine and five to two. Five minutes after nine and two they will not be admitted – also that if a child has been absent for a month it will not be admitted without a good reason given or a fine of a shilling'.

Emma said the women were 'quite tender hearted' after her few words and quite appreciated her wish to please and encourage them.

The third Dent legacy, which had been given to complete the restoration of the Chapel, had also been fulfilled, and the fully restored building was rededicated by Bishop Ellicott of Gloucester in August 1863. The next course was to find a suitable clergyman to take on the curacy, which John and Emma had agreed to support. The Bishop of Aberdeen put forward a suitable young man called Mr Robert Brown.

Emma was concerned at his youth, 'I should have liked one from his age and experience to whom I could have looked up. All thro' life I have been longing to find a friend on whom I might lean, who would be a help in spiritual things – it seems as if I am never to meet with an earthly prop'.

Robert Brown had not even been ordained at this time, and Emma entered into his subsequent ordination and first services at Sudeley in a very sentimental and obsessive fashion, almost as if she regarded him as her creation, referring to him as an 'offering which affects me infinitely more than did the re-opening of the Chapel – that was a gift of 'wood and stone' only – this seemed a dedication of soul and spirit'. He was to become one of her greatest disappointments when he left Sudeley after a year, ostensibly because of a disagreement with the choir, but more likely because he was smothered by Emma's expectations.

'Poor little Mr Brown – I think he is almost too excitable for his office – after dinner I fear I greatly annoyed him because I laughed when he gravely told me I was a Plymouth Brother. He is determined to leave – neither persuasion nor tears on my part have the slightest effect – I called upon him again late on Monday night after night school to beg him to make a fresh start – but he was like a rock', she said.

His successor was the 'formidable' Robert Noble Jackson, a much older and more experienced priest, who had formerly been a naval chaplain, and was promised an extra £50 a year above the Dent's stipend of £100 to encourage him to take the job. He never became the 'prop' which Emma was looking for but he was amusing company, and a great success at Sudeley at first.

He was particularly helpful to Emma when she wanted to use her legacy from William Brocklehurst's estate to build a new church at Gretton, and he soon became a valued travelling companion for her and John, acting as a private chaplain on some of their tours abroad.

Emma's diaries for these years are exhausting – so full of guests, organised entertainments, at homes, and croquet parties, as well as her teaching and work for the poor – that one is tempted to advise her, as her doctor did, 'not to work so hard and take life more quietly'. She remained dissatisfied.

'Oh how dull my journal is. I should like to record thoughts and feelings, sorrows and waking and sleeping dreams – it always seems to me that they constitute my real life – that everything else is quite unreal – but what I think about many things is so different to what others think – such different notions of right and wrong – of God – and of good prevailing that I often dread that some day I shall wake up to find all my notions are wrong and others right – my religion perhaps crumble away under my feet – and I stranded,' she wrote.

It was a great satisfaction to her to receive 'a most beautiful letter' from Florence Nightingale to thank her for sending the dried flowers she had gathered at Scutari. 'The little dried flowers she tells me are placed at the foot of her bed where she is now a constant prisoner – and the sight of them filled her eyes with tears of joy and would make her Xmas a day of thanksgiving – she says she is overwhelmed with Army business and the trying part of which is that she may never see the bodies and souls which the work is for, but my Scutari flowers are as it were a pledge to the eye of the spirit of our work – of our heroes lying at Scutari whose uncomplaining endurance she always strives to be worthy of'.

CHAPTER SEVEN

*P*ettit's Annual Diary for 1870 – the Second Year after Leap Year and the 33rd of the Reign of Her Majesty Queen Victoria.

Emma had relinquished her leather-bound journals for this small household diary, ready to record her travels in the East, when all their plans had to be cancelled after John splashed some heated ammonia into his eye, causing considerable damage – 'so here we are on the 1st January 1870 in horrid dirty London with very little prospect of our being out of the Drs. hands for weeks to come', she wrote. It was not going to be a happy year.

John had just recovered enough for them to escape to Brighton to visit her father when the news came from Macclesfield that her brother Henry had died. He had struggled for many years against ill-health – much of it the result of his difficult marriage. Emma described his exile from his home in London. 'What an agony it cost him to pass his own door, longing to see his children, yet dreading to see his wretched wife'.

Several thousand people turned out to line the

streets of Macclesfield for his funeral procession. As a former Mayor, he had been well-loved and respected in the town, and all the mill girls spent a portion of their weekly earnings buying crêpe and black rosettes to put on their bonnets for the occasion. Ann was too ill to attend, and she died later the same year, as if having plagued Henry through life she was determined to pursue him beyond the grave. Emma never even recorded her death, which left their six children orphaned. Maimie was already happily married to Gibbon Worthington and Johnny, Harry and Alfred were old enough to be absorbed by the Brocklehursts, but the two youngest children, Ernest then aged nine and Constance (Annie) aged seven went to live with Ann's brother, John Fielden at Dobroyd Castle, as he had no children of his own, and they were virtually brought up by him.

By May John was well enough to travel to the German spa at Ems to take the cure for his gout and rheumatism, while Emma took German lessons and played Bezique every evening. Mr Jackson, the new Sudeley parson, joined them at Baden Baden and they went on to attend a performance of the Passion Play at Oberammergau before they had to scramble home when France declared war on Prussia.

This was also just in time for Emma to be called to London where her father was dying. Although he had recovered from the stroke which he had suffered in 1861 he had never been able to fully resume his Parliamentary career, although his indulgent constituents had elected him in his absence in 1865. Since then the family had managed to persuade him that he should give up his seat,

and finally in 1868 'failing strength attendant on
advanced years rendered his retirement inevitable,
after 36 years earnestly promoting the interests of his
fellow-townsmen and his work people'. He had served
under three Prime Ministers, Melbourne, Palmerston
and Lord John Russell and had twice refused the
baronetcy offered to him.

After his death in London his body was taken north
to Macclesfield, where once again thousands of
mourners lined the route for the funeral procession to
Prestbury Church, and all the shops in the town were
closed for the day as a mark of respect. Emma's three
brothers, her husband and five grandsons were the
chief mourners as 'Time and the Grave closed over
one of the best of Fathers'.

Many years later Emma commissioned a marble
bust of her father which she presented to Macclesfield
Town Hall, together with a bound and printed *In
Memoriam* book, detailing his life and achievements,
which she sent to the mayor and councillors, as well
as to other leading people in the town.

Aunt and Uncle Tom also died during the year,
and Emma became obsessed with thoughts of her
own mortality. 'None of the Dent family left, but
John and I – we *ought* to be good and kind to one
another. When I feel cross and impatient this thought
calms me – the *last* of a family – I grieve over
it sometimes for my husband's sake – but for my own
it does not seem worth a thought – the waves of life
roll on so rapidly – none left to regret, that is better
than dishonour – but I may die soon – and John may
marry again and the name be continued – indeed
I often think how very soon my life may be ended – in

four years I shall be about as old as my mother and aunt were when they died – why should I live longer? This thought often occurs to me with immense force in the quiet of the night – four years, it seems so short a time to look forward to, and the feeling of how much I should like to do before I go is *overwhelming*'.

The once 'happy and united' Brocklehurst family seemed to be falling apart. Emma felt she had already 'lost' Marianne, who had turned her interest in photography into a professional one, and acquired a partner, Mary Booth, who was also to become her lifelong companion. Emma had discovered how close they were when she joined them on a photographic trip in Scotland a few years earlier. 'Marianne and Miss Booth seemed so all in all to one another. I felt quite cross and jealous and it required great determination to 'smother' the nasty little mean green-eyed monster. I wonder if it is only natural, or whether it is very bad in me to have such feelings – we used to be all in all to one another and now I am quite the third'. Marianne had for some time been signing herself MB and with the addition of Mary Booth they became known as the MBs. She later used her legacy from Uncle William to build Bagstones – a house on Philip's Swythamley estate for the two of them – Emma having characteristically used her share to build a new church at Gretton.

This was an era of passionate religious controversy, with the differences between the various factions of the church often leading to fierce antagonism, which perhaps helps to explain the fight which developed between the Dents and their former friend and curate, Mr Jackson, when after being promoted to Vicar of Winchcombe, he appointed a 'ritualist' as the new curate for Sudeley and Gretton. John complained to the Bishop about this 'Romanism' and was able to have him removed, but it was the start of a feud with Mr Jackson which was to run for the rest of their lives.

Emma caused the next rumpus by taking over the King's School after the death of Mr Cunningham, and directing that in future the Catechism should be dispensed with and religious instruction consist only of scriptures and explanation. On being told this over luncheon Mr. Jackson 'lost his head and was very abusive, not on *the question* at all – but on having accepted Winchcombe living three years ago – to please me – and now he is, he says, hundreds of pounds out of pocket – poor Revd Noble Jackson – I am sorry to say he is another example of the uncertainty of men having been admirable in one position being unable to bear a promotion to power,' Emma reported.

The final skirmish occurred when Mr Jackson began burying the dead and omitting the 'sure and certain hope of resurrection' from the service. John Dent asked if he would read it over him at Sudeley – he said "No!", 'which led to much that was very unpleasant'. Eventually, after letters from the Bishop, the vicar gave out from the pulpit that henceforth he would read it over everyone – as the words refer to the general resurrection, not to the individual, otherwise he could not say them. 'How incredible it seems that a man of 50 should retain such uncharitable and cruel views', Emma commented.

The Cheltenham Examiner reported on the unfolding story. 'There is a little ecclesiastical difficulty in the neighbouring city of Niniveh. The dominant family in the neighbourhood are not very much enamoured of the *noble* clergyman who performs at the adjacent rectory and therefore when he takes duty at the church, the family do not put in an appearance in the 'state box'.

'Last Sunday morning when the Communion was being administered by the Rector the family went to the other church, which so incensed the Rector that he refrained from administering the Sacrament, the more especially as one of the female villagers had giggled outright while he was forcibly impressing on his hearers the discord and 'hell upon earth' which is produced by bad-tempered husbands.'

The giggler was one of Emma's maids at what was considered to be a comment on the Dent's marriage, although by this time the relationship seemed to have overcome some of its earlier problems and to have settled into amiable companionship, with John being constantly referred to as 'my dear husband'. The sad sentiments of Emma's earlier poem: 'Strangers Yet?' with its lines 'After travel in far lands/After touch of wedded hands/ Why thus joined? Why ever met?/If they must be strangers yet?' appear to have been forgotten.

For his part John had recently given her a pair of long diamond earrings with the following note:

'My dear Nem,
    I'm quite aware that you will have said – Oh my goodness – I didn't want them – What a deal of

good might have been done with the money, and
diverse other exclamations, but at any rate now
you've got 'em you must wear them. I don't think
you have any fit for the representation of Marie
Antoinette, so when you are *en grande* tour they will
look bright and sparkling, and if I see them they
will remind me of my birthday and perhaps a flash
will come across me that we are not likely to see
together another 26 years.'

His reference to Marie Antoinette was to Emma's
supposed likeness to the French queen which was
often remarked on.

She now found herself playing marriage broker
again – this time for Edith, her favourite niece
and goddaughter. George Talbot, whose father was
Vicar of Withington, wanted to marry her, 'but he
has so little and William not inclined to do very
much, I fear it will have to fall through – but we must
hope for the best as we all like him very much and
Edith is much taken with him'. Both Emma and her
brother Peter interceded with William until he agreed
to meet George's family, with power from Edith to
decide as he thinks best. 'Clever little woman',
commented Emma. The outcome was that William
promised Edith a handsome allowance of £1,000 a
year 'and the young people are to have an interview
and talk over their own affairs and let him know if
they think it will do'.

They were married at Sudeley and the following
year Emma was with them at Prescott when Edith's
baby was born – 'how glad we were to hear his first
little cry. Prescott was a little Paradise – the garden

full of roses – the happy husband so grateful for Edith's safety – so proud of his newfound treasure'.

Emma's brother Peter had always been the odd one out in John Brocklehurst's family. He had opted for law rather than the silk trade and followed Uncle William into his legal firm and in the management of the Brocklehurst Bank. On their father's death he had inherited the family home at Hurdsfield and was now causing a great deal of anxiety over his proposed marriage to Dora Gaskell of Ingersley. William was particularly 'deeply vexed' at the possible connection.

'For years I have slaved at my post from a sense of duty which seemed somehow or other to have devolved upon me, and which seemed to become my legacy when father was first struck down by illness – God knows I have pulled at the oar ever since, and have made no end of sacrifices and discarded a life which would have been much more to my tastes and feelings than the one I have led – And now one's path is to be crossed at every turn by the slimy trail of people who have not a kind or sympathetic trait in their composition', he complained to Emma.

Peter called the engagement off at the eleventh hour – much to everyone's relief – and went off on a tour of the Continent. It was his only attempted excursion into matrimony and he died a bachelor. More significantly this marked the end of Hurdsfield House as the welcoming 'dear old family home' and the festive Christmas hearth. Emma and John were never invited there again and although she was never actively prevented from returning home the lack of invitation hurt her deeply.

In April 1875 Emma underwent a major operation,

which was probably a hysterectomy, and she was able to make use of her convalescent time at Eastbourne to continue writing her *Annals of Winchcombe and Sudeley*, a collection of historical facts which she had been working on for several years and hoped to turn into a book. She had met John Murray, the publisher, some years earlier through John's legal friend Mr William Cooke, and, with much encouragement from her husband, she sent him the completed manuscript for his advice.

'A creditable performance for any lady, but not calculated for general circulation', was his response, 'indeed I do not in my hands at least think I would obtain a sale for 40 copies'. However he detailed the cost of the proposed illustrations, and suggested that she might consider divorcing Sudeley from Winchcombe, and producing a smaller volume.

'Keeping the account of Sudeley separate from Winchcombe had occurred to me', she wrote, 'but the two are so united I did not know which was the most interesting or whether I should leave one out in the cold. If desirable the whole might be curtailed – but before doing anything will you kindly tell me what would be the cost, in addition to the illustrations, of printing 300 or 200 copies as it is (with slight omissions) folio size, in ordinary binding? And whether when corrections are made you would undertake to print it, of course entirely on our responsibility'.

'The undertaking is I know quite beyond my poor capabilities – and I have felt all along I ought not to have attempted anything of the kind – on the other hand so many who come regret there is no history of the place, and have urged me to put together in one volume all the information I have extracted from my husband's books – so that having gone so far in the work I would willingly go further both in trouble and expense (as my husband advises) if by so doing it could in any way be made worth publishing'.

John Murray rose to the occasion and the *Annals of Winchcombe and Sudeley* was published in 1877 – with 120 Portraits, Plates and Woodcuts – at a price of forty-two shillings. He had persuaded Emma to omit 'dear' before Husband and 'your affectionate Wife' from the Preface, otherwise there were few amendments. Kind and complimentary reviews appeared in *The Guardian*, *The Morning Post*, *Athenoeum* and the local Gloucestershire and Worcestershire papers. Only the reviewer in *The Academy* wrote what Murray described as a 'venomous' one, which wound up with the sentiment that it must be satisfactory to those who have no castles to restore that such work may be done by those who have not the power to describe them.

Emma, enjoying the adulation of her friends and letters of congratulation from among others Dr. Bully, headmaster of Cheltenham College, Lord Beauchamp and Hertford, the Bishop of Gloucester and Amelia B Edwards the writer, decided she disliked book reviews, particularly those on the *Annals* which were 'far too complimentary on the one hand, and venomously severe on the other – showing injustice in both ways'.

Meanwhile the great excitement in Winchcombe was the election of its first School Board, created after the Education Act in 1871. According to John Oakey political feeling ran high at the time and the Church and the Conservatives fought the Nonconformists and the Liberals for control of the schools. 'The excitement positively roused Winchcombe into life for several hours', Emma reported. 'A cold snowy day prevented me recording my votes as a ratepayer. The Vicar (Mr Jackson) and Brain were the weakest candidates and expected to fail, so great efforts were made for them and they were brought in well' (they headed the poll). 'John, supposed to be more than safe and expected to be head of the poll was nearly sacrificed' (coming second last).

Emma was beginning to flag in her efforts to provide almost continuous entertainments. 'I began to get to work in good earnest over the theatricals – and very hard work it is writing and planning everything and inviting everybody. How glad I shall be when it is all over – I often have my doubts if I am doing right in getting up these amusements and think I might be spending my time more profitably' she wrote.

Then there was the endless fund raising – not just for local Sudeley and Winchcombe projects. The Columbia Mission, the Protestant Church in Naples, the Jewish Mission in Constantinople run by her friends the Newmans, the Bishop of Antigua's endowment of his Bishopric – were just some of the many causes she was supporting. 'What hard work it is begging and how few respond' she commented. She began keeping note of how many letters she wrote and between March 1869 and October 1870 they totalled more than 1600.

She had been sad to hear of the death of Sir Thomas Phillips, who had become famous for amassing the greatest collection of books and manuscripts ever gathered together. They had enjoyed visiting him in the 1850s when he was living at Middle Hill outside Broadway where he also established a private printing press. Emma recalled one visit there: 'A few chairs were cleared of books for our accommodation – every corner crammed with books – pictures – Mss – Lady P obliged to sit in her bedroom and receive her lady friends – the billiard room crammed – coach house fallen in – the bell pull came out nearly a yard – we lunched in the housekeeper's room, passing thro' the kitchen – but what literary treasures we saw'.

Emma later considered having her own printing press at Sudeley but when on investigation this proved too difficult she compromised in 1882 by buying an American typewriter for £21 and was soon hard at work on it – 'Very much interested in my new plaything – the American typewriter – accomplished three pages of my Sudeley catalogue' she reported.

CHAPTER EIGHT

'As I went to the morning Sunday School the Castle field looked powdered with gold – the buttercups had opened all their leaves before the first really summer's sun – I gave my girls a lesson on law-duty-work-industry-talent . . . A dreary sermon from the Vicar on 'the rich man and Lazarus'- not much hope for the rich – not much for the poor. It was a relief to get out of church again into the beautiful air', Emma wrote.

Summer was always the best time at the Castle – John often went to Ems, the German spa, for his gout and rheumatism, while Emma enjoyed the company of her 'noble neighbours'. A new generation of Sudeleys were at Toddington 'making the place quite cheery' and Lord Elcho and his family came to Stanway. Emma was particularly fond of Lord Elcho's company. 'There is a great charm to me in being with distinguished people', she wrote, 'the more so of necessity here, we see so few – and in a thin and scattered neighbourhood like this I know of nothing so refreshing as having a few fresh spirits among us.'

However, the seemingly 'golden' summers came to an end in 1879, which historians describe as the worst recorded in modern times. 'It rained continuously' said Arthur Bryant in his *English Saga*. 'Everywhere the harvest blackened in the fields and farmers were faced with ruin, landlords with depleted rentals – three million sheep died of rot'. At Sudeley Emma recorded 'Six or seven cattle died on the estate – rotten like the sheep'. On May Day it snowed and throughout August they were glad of fires and she was still wearing her winter dress. On 29 August 'the first wasp I have seen this cold summer came bursting in as if he did not know where he was or how to make the most of his time', she wrote. They abandoned their plans to go abroad – 'John is very anxious about his farmers and we both think it is our duty to remain in England'. The weather improved eventually, but a run of disastrous harvests and the introduction of cheap imported food spelt the beginning of the end of prosperity for the great country estates.

Fortunately there was one good day that particular summer, when Emma hosted a visit from the Bristol and Gloucester Archaeological Society who had invited her to give a paper for their meeting at Sudeley. 'Decline to have anything to do with preparing a paper', she wrote 'but say that my experience of archaeologists is that on these occasions they arrive hot, dusty, dirty, tired, hungry and thirsty, not coming so much for the past as the present. I will have fresh meats ready for them, but not a paper'.

In the event 'nearly all went over the house, except Sir William Guise, who asked to retire to have a snooze and a pipe. I arranged the Castle as a mousetrap – they all went in at the front hall door and out by the servants' hall after writing their names in the travellers' book – friends took charge of each room, so that there was someone to explain everything that required explanation at every corner'.

Emma was still adding to the treasures at the Castle. A Mr George Barnard, of the Bank of England sent her a piece of lace which had been handed down through his wife's family, the Lawsons, who claimed to be descended from Katherine Parr. The lace was reputed to have been worked by Anne Boleyn, and to have been the lace canopy carried over Princess Elizabeth at her christening. Emma paid £25 for it and was delighted to discover that the falcon on a golden perch with roses, which was worked in the lace, was Anne Boleyn's crest, and she later had this verified by Mr George Hallis of the South Kensington Museum.

Another valuable addition to the treasures in the Queen's Room was a brooch containing some of Katherine Parr's hair. This was presented to the Castle by Miss Maggs to whom it had been bequeathed by Miss Durham of Postlip. Her brother had been one of the band who had broken open the Queen's coffin in 1792 – the hair in the brooch having been cut from the Royal remains at the time.

Emma continued with her plans for a small museum at Sudeley. 'The billiard table is converted into a first rate museum table. I have put all the skulls together in a little case, those from Australia are tiny in contrast with the Europeans'. A small grinding mill had arrived from Jerusalem, beside many other unusual objects, and her friend Mrs Newman of the

Jewish Mission in Constantinople had sent Bulgarian, Turkish and Circassian ornaments bought from the refugees in the city. Emma herself collected interesting objects from her travels – from Antwerp, which she had visited recently – she brought back a carving in wood 300 years old and a quaint hourglass with ironwork. Rare Chinese stamps were sent by Edith Allen from Shanghai, and 'Cousin Tom being in America kindly sends me stamps for my collection – some obtained from General Hazen, the head of the post office department – some are 'specimen stamps' and therefore unique. He says there is nothing worth buying in America, which is a comfort, except some Indian scalps lately taken from the heads of Sitting Bull's tribe by the Sioux.'

Cousin Tom, in between touring the world several times, had become Mayor of Macclesfield and High Sheriff of Cheshire – news of which prompted Emma to comment by quoting Webster's lines 'A sense of duty pursues us ever it is omnipresent like the Deity' – not, as some have suggested, referring to herself, but to the Brocklehurst family's penchant for public service. Cousin Tom is also reputed, rather less praiseworthy, to have introduced the grey squirrel to Britain, importing a pair from America for his Henbury Hall estate.

Emma was beginning to make her mark on Winchcombe. With Drayton Wyatt, the architect who had been Gilbert Scott's assistant on the Chapel, the Almshouses and Dents School, and John Oakey, the builder, she restored and enlarged the Jacobite House, opposite the parish church and built the Three Gables house in Gloucester Street.

At the time there were nearly twenty ale houses in the small town, and she was determined to do something about addressing the obvious problems. Mr Edgar Flower, a brewer from Stratford-on-Avon had recently bought the George Inn and The Gate public house and Emma approached him with a plan to turn one of them into a temperance inn. She would have preferred The George but 'all Winchcombe seemed to rebel against it being closed' and in the end she opted for The Gate which she opened as a coffee tavern, free to the members of the working mens' institution. Although she referred to it as her 'White Elephant', The Gate was well patronised by some of the young men 'and both my coffee taverns are prospering' she reported. She had earlier started a penny bank for the big boys 'to encourage them to put their pence in the bank instead of into the beer' and had changed the rooms for paying the road men from the public house to the coffee tavern, where they came in large numbers to receive their money, and many had hot cocoa and bread and butter instead of beer.

On the landmark side she had persuaded Mr Flower to let Drayton Wyatt restore the Pilgrim's Gallery at the George Inn at her expense (£76) and when Mr Agg Gardner, who had bought the White Hart Inn, was going to pull it down and replace it with a 'grand stone frightful vulgar building' she succeeded in persuading him to build the present black and white building instead. 'The design is not out of keeping with the Winchcombe surroundings and I hope sooner or later the Winchcombites will be grateful' she said.

We know that they were not. Emma records having a long conversation with her housekeeper Elizabeth Bayliss on the subject. 'I said how I had loved, prayed for, worked for and *devoted* myself to Winchcombe – and I did not think there was any love in return. She said when Prince Albert was alive no-one thought anything of him – now he was dead enough could not be said in his praise. I thought it was a very pretty way for a servant to put it'.

To her great sorrow Emma was soon to lose the faithful Bayliss, who had been her personal maid and also latterly her housekeeper for thirty years. She had been ill for some time, probably with consumption, and Emma arranged for her to be cared for in a nursing home in Bournemouth, where she stayed at Christmas to be near her and visited her every day. When she died shortly after this her body was brought back to Winchcombe where she was buried in St Peter's churchyard.

'I am obliged to seek a new housekeeper – Mrs Short comes with a year's character, but it is a great trial to bring a stranger into the very heart of our little ménage', Emma said. The little ménage at the time consisted of a butler, footman, housekeeper, cook, ladies maid, two housemaids and two kitchen maids, which seems a modest staff for a home the size of Sudeley Castle.

It was about this time that Emma began, somewhat eccentrically, wearing a pedometer to calculate her total annual mileage. In 1879 she recorded she walked 1140 miles and entertained nearly 1,000 extra people for breakfast, luncheon, dinner and tea.

John was now past sixty and becoming concerned with finding a suitable heir to inherit the Castle and estate. As they had no children, and he was the last of the line in the Dent family, his choice fell on Emma's Brocklehurst nephews, particularly Henry's two eldest orphaned sons, Johnny and Harry, both now officers in the Army.

Johnny was the brighter of the two and Emma's favourite. When he first came to stay at Sudeley she was full of admiration for this 'curious and somewhat interesting specimen of the Tribe of the Royal Horse Guards. Clothes superlative – boots – oh ye gods what fits! What expanse of shirt front when dressed for dinner – how careful at dinner not to partake of fattening food! I was afraid he was not well, but his Uncle Dent said 'it was only d—affectation'.'

Then there was general approval in the family when he became engaged to Miss Louisa Alice Parson, eldest daughter of the Hon Laurence and Mrs. Parson. William wrote to Emma:

'Everyone describes the bride elect as very ladylike – rather petite, rather delicate – just the sort to captivate a lad like Johnny and hold him in silken chains . . . The wedding is to take place at the end of February – they have rented a house at Windsor and propose to reside there for the next two years and the soldier will continue in the Army during that time. I think and hope he will remain till he gets his troop – the young lady will have a tidy fortune of her own which she will get on the death of her father who is 71'.

Johnny's obvious commitment to the Army, and the fact that over the next three years he and Louie had no children, influenced John towards Harry 'a smart young fellow enough' and to his mind more sober and suited to take over the Castle and estate. Also the fact that Harry had been christened Henry Dent ensured the continuity of the Dent name. He was even more certain that he had made the right decision when in 1881 Harry married Marion Lascelles, daughter of the Hon Egremont Lascelles of Middlethorpe Hall near York, and the following year when he and Emma were at Aix-les-Bains a telegram came from Harry 'Marion got boy this afternoon both doing well'. The succession of Sudeley was assured.

Emma did not share John's enthusiasm for Harry's wife, Marion, and regretted the fact that she had made Harry give up steeple-chasing. 'He is never going to ride in one again, which is good of him as he has been winning some national races lately, and been much complimented in the papers for his cool head and hands and temperate habits'. Instead Harry, with his customary good nature, left the Army and settled down to the life of a Yorkshire country gentleman, taking on the Mastership of the York and Ainsty Hunt.

There was more excitement in the family when Emma's youngest brother, Philip, who had been rattling around in Swythamley on his own since inheriting the house and estate from Uncle William, unexpectedly announced his engagement to a 'Cheshire rose' – Miss Annie Lee Dewhurst. 'Philip seems in a state of VIIth Heaven as is the case with most young lovers of 56', Emma commented.

'My good fortune astonishes me', he wrote to her, 'for I am shortly to marry a most charming young lady of 28 who in every possible way is qualified to make my old home as happy as a home can be. . . Miss Dewhurst's father is dead, but she possesses the dearest and kindest of old mothers and one most amiable younger sister – there are no more, the brother having died at Cambridge. Their estates in Cheshire and Wales are managed by Trustees, their uncles, Sir Henry Lee and another uncle a member of Parliament.' They were married quietly, with Cousin Tom as best man, and the only Brocklehurst to attend the ceremony.

'My, it is a go about PLB', commented Johnny from Egypt. 'She seems a bit young for him, but he knows his own business'. Colonel Gordon who had just been made Governor of the Sudan had 'taken an immense fancy' to Johnny and was trying to get him transferred to his staff. 'Gordon seems also to have taken a great liking to Marianne and Miss Booth', Emma wrote. They had met during the MB's excursions to Egypt, where they were now established Egyptologists, so much so that Gordon himself used to refer to them as 'the foreign office'.

How Emma envied Marianne her opportunities to travel to Egypt and the East, particularly now that through John's health she was confined to Europe, and even there to a succession of spas and health resorts. However, she did not share her liking for fishing, which had resulted in the MBs renting a cottage in Ireland to pursue this sport. 'Marianne writes they have caught in all 39 fish in Ireland – 415 lbs weight – and her feats are mentioned every week in *The Field*. What a strange taste for Marianne to have – I cannot understand how any *woman* can take pleasure in catching and killing any living thing', Emma commented.

She was always on the side of the animals, and became an active member of the RSPCA and the Anti-Vivisection Society – leaving a legacy of £1,000 to the latter society in her Will. But it was to her own animals that she became particularly devoted. When the Dents' Lyme mastiff Juno suffered from cancer of the bone and had to be put down, she upraided those who deplored her concern for 'Only a dog' and justified her feelings in a thirteen verse poem in praise of Juno, who was buried under the mulberry tree which she and Marianne had planted by the Dungeon Tower at Sudeley twenty years earlier.

Another favourite, their fox terrier Busy, was small and well behaved enough to travel everywhere with John and Emma – even to the Continent in the days before quarantine. On one occasion at Toulon station *en route* for Grenoble they met up with Johnny travelling back to London, who was looking out of his carriage window when he saw the back of Uncle Dent's head. 'He looked further and discovered the owner thereof in the extremely round person in the celebrated enormous topcoat which hid Busy in the sleeve – more remarkable on that day the heat being excessive and equal to July in England.'

Johnny spoke in enthusiastic terms of Colonel Gordon, whose Egyptian expedition he would have liked to join, but having been recalled by the Army, he was on his way home on board a troop ship, carrying 400 troops and forty Krupp steel guns, when the ship caught fire about 100 miles from Suez and the whole cargo of guns and ammunition was destroyed. Newspaper reports at the time said 'A young gentleman named Brocklehurst is said to have behaved very gallantly and was nearly drowned.'

'Three winters past we have been absent from the old château', Emma wrote, when they had either been in the South of France or at Brighton, where she found Mr Cockings' sermons at Holy Trinity Church particularly uplifting. The Cotswold winters in those days were severe. Emma describes one occasion when there was so much snow on the hills above the Castle that Mr Cox (the doctor) could not ride to see his round of patients, but had to walk 20 miles. 'On all sides we hear of accidents, loss of lives, trains stopped', she said. The Castle looked like a wedding cake in the drifting snow and rooks, pigeons, blackbirds, robins and sparrows all came 'to feed and quarrel' there.

At the end of 1884 they spent their first Christmas at Macclesfield for ten years, with no premonition that it was to be their last. The family party had shrunk to Peter, William and Mary, Fitz and Arthur, George and Edith Talbot, Alfred and themselves. The MBs were in Ireland and Johnny in far off Egypt, looking after hundreds of camels at a Remount Depot. Emma's annual mileage on the pedometer was 1144 miles, and before they left Sudeley, they had had all their cottagers to tea and given them their presents as usual – 'with others, including cottagers, making up about 100 presents has made me very busy', she said.

Her brother William had been having troubles of his own. Having inherited his father's Parliamentary seat in 1868, he was unseated in 1880 by the Bribery Commission, when they were called in to investigate the extreme excesses of the election campaign.

Although he and his fellow candidate were cleared by the judges of any discreditable conduct, his lawyers, Mair and May were sentenced to nine months imprisonment for their part in bribing the electorate.

As a result he was very 'down and out' and wrote to Emma saying he felt isolated compared to thirty or forty years earlier when they were a large united family 'and the elders still at the front. The ties seem to be loosening every year – the ground loosening under our feet – as if preparing to receive us'.

'Ah well a day, we must take life as we find it', Emma commented. 'Try to do no harm, as much good as we can, work as hard as we can. We shall be misunderstood and mischief made between rich and poor – as Gladstone is doing in his vanity and self-sufficiency – bringing troubles and destruction upon a class, which if left to themselves would do well enough – landlord and tenant – putting discontent and destruction between us'.

She and John had just returned to Sudeley from Brighton in March 1885 when John became ill.

'A very cold wind and he went on his cob to see Brain at Greet on the arrangements for the Conservative Meeting to be held on the 28th', Emma wrote. When he came back he looked very ill and complained of pain in his chest, and though a good night seemed to restore him, for the next few days he breakfasted in his room and completed a round of meetings – Magistrates, School Board, Dents School and Almshouses, as well as preparing and sending out the papers for the Conservative Meeting which he was to chair. 'We were very busy and happy and had hoped to get out of this cold climate to Brighton and perhaps to Italy, but alas the cruel hand of death was in the terrible cold wind and the end was at hand', Emma said.

The following day – 25 March – John was at his work and interviewing people till late in the afternoon, then he walked as far as Pardington's with the dogs, Duke and Busy. Everybody who met him said how ill he looked, but he seemed better at dinner, and he and Emma had a long talk about his will, heirs, property, nephews etc. Emma told him her scheme for a £10 deposit fund for the Almshouses, which he said was surrounded with difficulties, but that he had left a legacy of £5 to each inmate of the Almshouses for three years.

At 8.30 he went to the Study, and when Emma took Busy to him she said he was singing to himself – 'it sounded cheerful, but I have wondered since if it meant pain. At 9.30 he came into the Library, saying he was going to bed and sat down for a last chat as he often did, then he took up his bed-candle, saying he supposed I should not follow for two or three hours', Emma recalled. 'A few minutes after he knocked for me from his room above – I thought the knocking somehow different to usual and I rushed upstairs – he was rubbing favourite oils on his chest and complaining of a return of the pain which had seized him the previous week – after the oils he asked me to keep quite quiet, he said he was foolish to have gone out in the cold wind. I was very anxious to ring and tell someone to fetch the Doctor but was afraid to fidget him. He drew the bed clothes well over his shoulders, said he should soon be better when he was warmer. . . I remained quiet at the dressing table. He said 'Oh Nem this pain!'. He turned round as if to compose himself for sleep, gave one loud breathing which made me think he had fallen asleep, the second alarmed me, the third I looked at him, when alas, alas he was gone'.

'Before I left him that terrible night, I held his hand, so soon going cold, and knelt beside him vowing I would try to the very uttermost, with God helping me, to devote the remainder of my poor life to carrying out his wishes. I knelt and wept . . . and then the domestics and medical attendant led me to another room – for I did not wish to see him again prepared for the grave – I only wanted to think of him and remember him as he was in life – and those last days', Emma mourned.

He was buried in the family vault in the Chapel, and as was to be expected, Mr Jackson was barred from performing the burial service, which was conducted instead by the Rector of Toddington. There was a full if not fulsome obituary in the *Gloucestershire Chronicle*. 'He was Lord of the Manor of Winchcombe, chairman of the Winchcombe Petty Sessional division of magistrates and had been chairman of the Winchcombe District School Board since 1875. In politics he was a staunch Conservative, but his political views never warped his judgement or hindered his generosity'. His fellow magistrate Mr J. Waddingham said 'If faults he had – and who alas is without them – they were of the head, not of the heart, of the temper rather than the understanding, and served, as the setting does for the diamond, to enable his sterling excellencies of mind and heart to shine the more brilliantly.'

In his Will the castle was left for the use of Emma

in her lifetime and then 'after her decease to the use of Henry Dent Brocklehurst . . . during his life'. In a lengthy entailment John decreed that after Harry's death Sudeley would go to the use of his sons, and of their sons thereafter 'in tail male'.

With the Will Emma found his last letter to her on pink paper written in 1881:

'My dear Nem

I have again made a will – JFB has at present no children. HDB is going to be married – one could think he is likely to have some – I hope you will think I have made a fair and good will – I can assure you it has given me many hours thought – and it has been very difficult, as it is it has been done, I believe, in consonance with your wishes.– '

'I trust my successor will keep up old Sudeley well and hospitably. I hope that he will live here as much as he can, be a good and just landlord and I hope he will be 'true to the Banner Blue' and uphold the credit of my name as I have tried and make a much better man than your unworthy but affectionate husband.

John C. Dent

and May God bless you and watch over you all the days of your life.'

CHAPTER NINE

'I feel like the ivy we planted against the Castle walls, in a moment torn down by the blast in January – nothing can restore it', Emma wrote. 'Seven long sad months of utter loneliness, darkness, misery, sorrow – so suddenly to lose my dear husband, the constant companion of 38 years – now I have no one to live for, to consult – no one to live for me – no one to talk things over with. Oh it is a darkness that may be *felt*'.

She remembered how John had regretted his loss of friends and contact with her family – 'especially Marianne, whom he loved I think next best to me – none of them half appreciated him, neither brothers, sister, nephews or nieces. In my estimation he was superior to them all.'

That autumn Harry and his wife, and Johnny, who was now a Major, came to Sudeley for a few days shooting. 'Tho' I have been quite cheerful and apparently in good spirits they little think of the pain I felt in the depth of my heart in seeing his place filled by another', Emma said.

She was dismayed at Harry's decision to buy Roel farm and Spoonley, as John had always considered that Sudeley was better without any more land. 'I suppose, being young, game may have been the great attraction, but with the Lodge on my hands – the Water Hatch under notice – the Wadfield to follow, I have protested against buying another yard of land', she commented. As it turned out Harry had bought Roel to farm himself, feeling perhaps that he needed a personal stake in the estate which he was now due to inherit.

It was a doubtful decision, as agricultural conditions continued to decline, and Emma had already been faced with a deputation from her farm tenants, asking for a reduction in their rents. 'Our corn crops are in bad condition and unfit for the market. Stock of all kinds can only be sold at a great loss and sacrifice, while the expense of labour and taxation are as heavy as in better times', they pleaded.

She wrote to her brother William for advice, and he agreed that reductions in farm rents were being called for everywhere, with the value of land down nearly 50 per cent. He suggested encouraging the farmers to adapt themselves to the requirements of the times by turning from corn growing to grass and hay production, and rearing cattle. She could also help them with gifts of manure, which she should be able to get cheap from Cheltenham. 'It is a pity you have no railway handy or you might have any amount of good London stable stuff laid down at 5s a ton', he wrote, advising her against breeding rabbits which were already flooding the market.

Emma decided to try chickens. 'My incubator is in full force having hatched 70 out of 100 eggs', she reported.

'The little chickens are all flourishing round about the Castle'.

Political passions still ran high in Winchcombe and Emma, who felt particularly impelled to carry on the Dent's support for the Tories, upset the local Liberal opposition by writing a letter to each voter asking them to vote for the Tory candidate in the 1885 election. She reminded them of the interest her late husband had always taken in Winchcombe, and how anxious he would have been to see Mr Yorke returned. The Liberals, Swinburne and Sexty, took exception to this 'undue influence' and pasted copies of her letter up on their committee room windows, refusing her request to take them down. After a bitter contest the Tories won with a majority of 182 and Emma hoisted the blue flag at the Castle, but there remained a lot of bad feeling in the town, and several Tory supporters had one or more panes of glass broken in their windows, including those at the Vicarage.

Emma had already begun 'gerrymandering'. 'I have given Harry and his brothers votes in the Division – also to Mr Cripps – by selling them cottages in Vineyard Street', she wrote. These were some of the block of seven cottages on the west side of the street which she had bought in 1882 for £375. It is interesting to note that this behaviour was apparently not thought reprehensible at that time, although probably not met with much enthusiasm by her political opponents.

By the beginning of 1886 the brass plate in John's memory was ready to be put up on the Chapel wall with the words 'The Lord be between thee and me when we are parted one from another'. 'I wept all thro' the service and slept all thro' the sermon', Emma said.

'I am making up my mind to go abroad, but words cannot say how bitter it is to arrange only for myself – after all these years of life, when my one effort has been to forget self, it is heartaching to have now to do so. I am disappointed Peter will not go with me. He cannot make this one sacrifice for his sister, after all John's goodness to the family'.

She travelled on her own to Florence and the hotel where she and John had always stayed. 'How dreadfully lonely it seems – this misery is like a mental illness. My people have no idea what I am suffering, or one surely would have insisted, not to say offered, to have escorted me', she wrote.

Some respite came with Drayton Wyatt, the architect, full of plans for the new building at the Castle. 'Workmen are pegging out and preparing for the new West buildings', Emma wrote. 'A great undertaking for me all alone, but with Mr Wyatt to the front and the shadow of Sir Gilbert Scott in the background, I feel every stone will be in accordance with what my dear husband would approve.' (George Gilbert Scott had been knighted in 1872).

In Winchcombe Mr Wyatt had already extended the old Wesleyan Chapel in Cowl Lane to form the new Infants School after Arthur Smith had given the School Board notice to leave the building in Abbey Terrace, where the school had been housed. Emma had paid for the new building and agreed to let it to the School Board for seven years at £30 per annum.

She was also having central heating installed at Sudeley. 'Having had hot water introduced in the Castle (just in time) it makes the cold bearable', she wrote. 'I am living up in the study'. Work on the new buildings was at a standstill because of the frost. Work had also stopped on the restoration of the Roman villa which had been found in Spoonley Wood by David Hicks in 1883 -

'The Romans are gone into winter quarters', Emma wrote. The villa had proved to be larger than the one which had been discovered earlier at Wadfield, and she was determined that it should be carefully excavated and preserved. Clearing the wood and roofing the pavements with old Roman tiles found among the debris had already cost her £121 10s.

While it has been a particularly severe winter in England, Emma was glad that she had not gone to the South of France where a series of earthquakes had shaken the Riviera. Her cousins Jos and Ellen Fielden had been too ill to leave their rooms in Cannes when the shocks came, and their children would not leave their parents, even though all the other occupants of the hotel had fled into the garden. Ellen reported that the first shock was at 6 a.m., the second at 8 and another at 8.30 with a final one at 2 a.m. the following night. 'The panic in the hotel was I think worse than the actual shock' she said. 'I thank God he prevented my leaving home at this time'.

At home she was gradually starting to divest herself of some of her responsibilities. 'I decided to give up the School Board, but nominated W. Pardington in my place. I wrote to every voter stating that I thought the Parish should be represented and begged them to support him at the coming election – he was returned at the head of the poll.' But her political enemies in Winchcombe continued to taunt her.

'Last week at a public meeting Mr Jackson expressed a

wish that the old stocks, which I had preserved for the last few years, should be returned to Winchcombe – it was not nice in him to do so. Arthur Smith enquired if the sale of the Jacobite House to us ten years ago was legal and Mr Troughton enquired if the stocks were stolen. Nice trio!' Emma reported.

'I sent the stocks back to the Town Hall, and only hope they will be cared for. In the *Evesham Journal* I have explained how they were brought here for preservation, with the sanction of the then High Bailiff. The Jacobite House I offer to the Town for re-purchase'.

As if these were not problems enough, she was distressed to hear that William and Fitz had opened a democratic club in Macclesfield, whose aims included the abolition of the House of Lords in England and the establishment of a Parliament in Dublin. When she reproached William angrily he wrote 'I don't see why you should aim to do just what the old Dents and John would be supposed to wish' – and he went on to explain the changes which had taken place during the last few years. 'How such sentiments would have grieved them all, but in William and Peter, who not only thought it, but acted it. I am glad the name of Brocklehurst is not be held here' Emma decided, seeming not to realise that by denying her own radical upbringing she was becoming even further isolated from her family. She never went back to Macclesfield again.

As part of her never-ending tribute to the Dents, she was hanging the painting she had commissioned from Charles Cattermole, depicting Uncle William Dent starting as High Sheriff in 1851 to meet the Judges at Overbridge, accompanied by 300 friends, neighbours and tenants, with Uncles John and Benjamin Dent and her husband standing in the Castle doorway. 'I feel a pleasure in thinking how gratified the kind old man would have felt in knowing that wonderful day was immortalised in one of Cattermole's pictures', she lamented, now that there was now no-one to share her pleasure in the painting.

She had been generous in her patronage of the arts and she now commissioned the sculptor Holme Cardwell, who she and John had first met in Rome on their honeymoon tour, to make a bust from memory of her husband. He had earlier carved them a statue of Sabrina, the water nymph, for their first home at Severn Bank.

Josiah Rushton, the Worcester painter, was another of her favourite artists, and as well as portraits of John and herself, carried out many commissions for her, including copying the Sudeley portraits of the Dent Uncles for presentation to Worcester and Winchcombe Town Halls. Boulton, the Cheltenham sculptor, carved a full-length statuette of Queen Victoria and a bust of Emma's father for presentation to Macclesfield Town Hall, and he also made the statues of Henry VI and Queen Victoria which stand on either side of the West door of the Chapel at Sudeley.

Millais was a friend of hers, and she often used to visit his studio when she was in London and William F. Yeames – best known for his painting entitled *When did you last see your Father?*, duplicated his Royal Academy painting of the death scene of Amy Robsart to hang on the Castle walls.

For some time there had been a suggestion that St Kenelm's Well on the Sudeley estate could be used to provide tapped water for Winchcombe, and to commemorate Queen Victoria's Golden Jubilee in 1887

Emma decided to make this happen. A tablet in the Well's Conduit House states:

'In loving memory of the three brothers, John, William and the Rev. Benjamin Dent and also of their nephew, John Coucher Dent, water from this abundant and ever-flowing stream was conveyed as a free gift to the inhabitants of Winchcombe by Emma, widow of the above-named John Coucher Dent'. Among her bills she records that the cost to her was £375. The Winchcombe Rural Sanitary Authority then borrowed £1,000 from the Public Works Loan Board to meet the cost of installing mains for a domestic supply throughout the town.

'The Jubilee and the new water supply were marked by a splendid day of celebration' said the *Evesham Journal*. 'The day was ushered in with a peal of 1,887 changes on the Parish church bells, commencing at 6 o'clock in the morning . . . As the morning advanced the entire population seemed astir, clothed in their Sunday best, the glorious summer sunshine infusing a feeling of warmth and happiness into every heart . . . 'A thanksgiving service for the Jubilee was held in the parish church, after which everyone gathered in Abbey Terrace around the temporary fountain which had been erected for the ceremony of opening the Winchcombe Water Supply.

Mr Smith-Wood, the High Bailiff, then presented Emma with an address which had been signed by all the householders in the town and engrossed in Old English on vellum, beautifully illuminated, with the impression of the ancient seal of the borough in colours. He was followed by Ada Balfour Noble Jackson, the Vicar's small daughter, who gave her a bouquet of choice white flowers, adding at the same time 'Thank you very much for the water'.

In her reply Emma said: 'I hope you all believe what a really sincere pleasure it has always been to me to take part in anything relating to the good of Winchcombe. How for 40 years you and your interesting old town have ever been in my best thoughts and how it was the great wish of those who are gone to leave an influence for good and not for evil among you. I seem to stand here today as their representative, and in their name and to their memory, present you with what I know you all value and which I hope both now and in years to come will remind you of good men and true'.

She then touched a small lever near at hand and 'instantly a stream of water, pure as crystal, leaped high into the air, amid loud clapping of hands. The band then played the National Anthem, which was taken up by all present, and so the ceremony ended.'

Later in the day 500 of Winchcombe's inhabitants sat down to a 'meat tea' at her invitation, and the girls of the day and Sunday schools were each given a Jubilee medal and a new shilling. Emma had more than 700 medals cast for the occasion to be distributed among the people and children. In the evening a 30 ft Jubilee bonfire was lit on Langley Hill.

Amid all the rejoicing Emma felt the lack of any member of her family, to support her at the ceremony, particularly the absence of Harry and Jack. 'I stood all *alone*', she said. 'How few know the depth of that little word'.

To make up for her disappointment, the following month Harry and Marion brought the five-year-old Jack on his first visit to the Castle which would be his one day. Emma declared him, 'A little darling, beautiful, good mannered and a little gentleman. I thought what a pleasure it would have been for dear John to have seen him'. She still had rather an uneasy relationship with Marion, who had understandably vetoed the suggestion that she and Harry should move to Sudeley and share the Castle with Emma, and even appeared to resent any time Harry spent away from Yorkshire at Roel and Sudeley, so she was pleased when Marion wrote from Acombe: 'I want to thank you very much for your kindness to Jack and I hope as he grows older he may be a pleasure to you'.

Some of the Winchcombe worthy citizens sent Emma a petition requesting her to agree to have her portrait painted, and placed in the Town Hall to commemorate her gift of water to the town, but she declined, saying she had 'an insurmountable objection to sitting for a portrait and I fear I could never consent to be placed in such a conspicuous position'.

In the meantime she was very busy at Sudeley, building an entrance lodge (the North Lodge), planting a maze, taking in the Grange (the Tithe Barn), levelling all the ground, widening the moat four yards, planting thirty cedars 15 ft high, and putting a terrace all round the moat. This could only be done by removing the field, which was the same level as the terrace -and in doing this many interesting fragments were found – Roman flints, coins, stirrups, stags horns etc.

More than 2,000 people came to the annual Flower Show at the Castle that summer – 'a lovely day and the improvements all looked their best' and the wife of one of the committee members wrote afterwards: 'I know what pleasure it is to you, having such a delightful home to impart some of its charms to us poorer people, and I am sure dear Madam, that such times, such as yesterday, draws all our hearts nearer to you and binds such a cord round us as shall not easily be broken'.

But Emma continued to be lonely beyond expression. Her friend Bessie Calrow, writing in the Cheltenham Ladies College magazine said, 'perhaps her friends felt she wrapped herself up in her loneliness and would not allow anyone to sympathise – my own feeling was that it was her great unselfishness; she felt each had her duties, or perhaps a busy life of work, and she would not take them from it just for her pleasure. If the unutterable loneliness in that great place was heavy, it was part of her burden, and she must carry it to the end'.

We know that three years after John's death she had a chance to remarry. Pasted in her diary is a page of lines by Dean Stanley and beside them she wrote: 'These beautiful lines came from one who had known me long and now urged me to be his wife – for a few hours I hesitated, it was a temptation to go out of my utter loneliness into the sunshine and be surrounded by love and sympathy – but two years my junior and his wealth and position seemed likely to bring upon me more responsibilities, and of these I already have too many – forsaken by those I could have most leaned upon, Wm and Mary, the Talbots, and shut out from my own dear old home thro' the caprice of a cruel, selfish brother – it does not bear thinking of'.

The identity of this admirer remains a mystery. The description does not seem to fit any of Emma's friends or acquaintances, nor is the handwriting familiar, and as the inscription has been so heavily scored over by her that it is illegible, she obviously intended it to stay a secret.

Peter, the 'cruel and selfish brother' referred to, did finally invite her to the old family home at Hurdsfield one Christmas, but in her bitterness she said his invitation came too late after twelve or thirteen years and she could not go. Instead she chose to go to Swythamley, where her brother Philip and his wife Annie and their three children cheered her out of her 'dark loneliness' and she spent several of the following Christmases with them.

Women's suffrage was an important topic of the day, and while women were still without a vote for Parliament, in 1889 they were able to vote for the first time in the County Council elections. Emma took advantage of this to publish a political 'flyer' which she sent to all her 111 'sister' voters in Winchcombe, urging them to vote for the Tory candidate, Lord Elcho. 'My little circular brought down anathemas from the other side, anonymous letters and much abuse', she reported.

'Lord Elcho worked hard, but Swinburne and party told lies by the dozen – promised they should have no more rates and taxes and goodness knows what else besides. According to the Registers and promises there were 54 traitors, Lord Elcho lost by 20 votes, and to the perpetual disgrace of Talbot, Waddingham Junior etc. they supported Swinburne'. Emma was particularly angry with Edith's husband, George Talbot, for his betrayal after she had given him the vote by buying him a cottage at Dursley (price £50) with a promise from him always to vote blue 'and on the Conservative side'.

Her political circular had been published by William Belcher, who set up the first printing press in Winchcombe, and this gave her all the encouragement she needed to start her own local magazine, with the aim of encouraging people to take an interest in the history of their town and neighbourhood. The first issue of the *Winchcombe and Sudeley Record* was published in January 1890, price one halfpenny, and Mr Belcher reported that his little shop was quite besieged for copies. Having warned her readers that it was up to them whether the 'experimental leaflet' would succeed or fail, Emma continued to produce it monthly until December 1896, sprinkling the announcements of births, deaths and marriages among a collection of local superstitions (which ran for sixteen issues), histories of the post office, the fire engine and the waterworks, and learned articles about the Roman villa at Spoonley and the excavations of Winchcombe Abbey.

Independent of the *Record* she was also collecting for a Professor Sidgwick answers to the psychological question – 'Have you ever seen, heard or felt anything for which you could not account' – and out of 200 answers she had already recorded thirty-six curious and interesting experiences.

'It was six months after her husband's death that a cataract began to form upon her eyes', Bessie Calrow wrote. 'A trial peculiarly hard to her, especially in the work she set herself, which involved so much reading and writing' – not just the *Record* but also some 400 letters a year.

'I never heard her complain, save saying how slow it made her in getting through, and it caused her to sit up so late at night, as she often had to rest her eyes by closing them—She with her dear faithful dogs often sat far into the night and she had many stories to tell of her surprising the watchman on his rounds, and holding conversations with him through door or window, to his great entertainment'.

She was to lose both her favourite dogs in the following years. 'My poor dear faithful Duke (Juno's successor) went to the Happy hunting ground', Emma recorded. 'Who can say how I shall miss him and his loving welcome. He was too big for the parlour, so never admitted in former times, but strange to say the first day I came down after my dear husband's death, he pushed his way in and came and laid his head on my knee, as if full of sympathy and love. They buried him under the mulberry tree'. Later the same year Busy the fox terrier followed – 'for 14 years the little faithful creature was seldom out of my sight, now both my best friends are gone', she wrote.

Then as birthday followed birthday with no wishes or remembrances from family or friends 'the grave has robbed me of all my love'. An obituary on Jenny Lind reminded her of how she and John had enjoyed her singing. 'We were never very extravagant in our pleasures, but I remember on one occasion we paid £5 each for stalls to hear in *Roberto*'.

Fortunately she did have some new friends - particularly Dorothea Beale, the Principal of Cheltenham Ladies College. 'She is very learned and pleasant and good company', Emma wrote, and when she came to stay at Sudeley 'Amuses herself all morning, breakfasts in her own room and then walks for an hour, so in a sensible way we do not meet till luncheon'. Girls from the College were often entertained at the Castle, among them Victoria Davies, Queen Victoria's African godchild, who sometimes spent part of her school holidays with Emma.

Drayton Wyatt, the architect was a great consolation, and with his help and encouragement she was continuing to make improvements at Sudeley. John Oakey, the builder who worked on all her projects said 'For many years a good deal of labour was employed at the Castle, local labour always where possible' and Dorothea Beale remembers Emma remarking with pleasure, 'They say now no one will be out of work in Winchcombe for the whole winter'.

In 1887 she had added the new West gateway to the Castle and adjoining buildings, now called the Jubilee building, and later a covered way was built across the quadrangle, to connect the old with the new buildings. The stable yard was extended with underground chambers for coal, coke, wood and rubbish – 'John always said we must not have a back door to the Castle.'

The final addition was the North Tower, to replace an earlier one which is shown on drawings of the original Castle. It was completed in July 1890. 'It looks very new now – quite an eyesore', Emma said, 'but in a very few years it will be toned down and be a great improvement to the Castle.'

More ambitiously, she decided to revise a scheme suggested by Gilbert Scott some forty years earlier – to build a new road from Winchcombe to Sudeley, approaching the Castle down what was then called Duck Street. 'As to that Duck of a Street – do you think that any cobwebs have been found across it?' queried Drayton Wyatt. 'I am rather disposed to regard the scheme as a hopeful one'. He and Emma had an interesting time planning the two bridges that would be needed, first making them out of wood to see what they would look like, then to more detail, 'stones lying about in all directions, seemingly a hopeless mass of stuff for ever putting into shape.' Emma wrote. When preparing the foundation for the first new bridge at the bottom of Duck Street, John Oakey, the builder, found the stump of the old ducking stool, which was used for the ducking of refractory women. Although he was a staunch Liberal, and was once sacked by her for expressing his radical views, Emma soon re-instated him because of the value of his work, and he and Drayton Wyatt made a very successful team.

To her great sadness Drayton Wyatt died before their last project was completed. 'I have lost my best friend,' Emma wrote. 'For the last six years he has been friend, advisor, brother, far more considerate than any relatives – the last line is snapped and broken which connected with the past, all the work that has been done for the last 36 years'. On her own she put the cap stone on the second bridge over the lake and decided on the size of the balls – 'but I still think they are not quite right', she said.

In May 1895 Emma went to London, where Mr Nettleship, who had recently performed the same operation on Mr Gladstone, removed the cataract from her right eye. 'A beautiful and painless operation. I watched every movement and was delighted to see a speck of blue light as soon as it was cleared,' she said. 'I was allowed to come home in a fortnight. They rang the church bells for my happy return and success of the operation – it was intended kindly, but it was ill-judged. The country was exquisite after our small cramped rooms in London. It was a lovely afternoon when all the inmates of the Dents Almshouses came to tea, the air full of sweet scents and hawthorn'.

CHAPTER TEN

On a dismal February morning in 1900 a solitary mourner met the train at Woking, bringing the last remains of Emma Dent to the crematorium. It was Harry who had the melancholy and lonely task of attending her cremation, and then transporting her ashes in an oak casket back to Winchcombe, where they were placed in the family vault in the Chapel at Sudeley.

Emma's request for cremation at a time when it had only recently become legal, and the only crematorium was at Woking, might have been considered perverse, but was typical of her progressive and curious nature. Her friend Dorothea Beale, who shared many of her religious ideas, was to follow her example when she died six years later, and it seems possible that they may have discussed the subject together after the Cremation Society had been founded in 1884.

The logistics of carrying out her wish were never discussed and it was left to Harry to make all the necessary arrangements.

The last entry in her diaries was in December 1896,

when her pedometer was still recording an annual mileage of over 1200 miles and she had entertained more than 2,000 guests to breakfast, luncheon, dinner and tea. Her remaining years after that are not chronicled, but we know that in August 1899 she had a serious illness which left her more or less permanently bedridden. *The Cheltenham Examiner* in its report of her death said: 'Her serious illness – born with cheerfulness had been relieved by intervals of comparative freedom from pain and she had then, in bright weather, been wheeled out in the grounds of the Castle she loved so well. By careful nursing and attention, promises seemed to be given that she would escape any serious consequences from the rigours of winter, but about 10 days ago she developed symptoms of influenza and bronchitis and despite all that medical skill could do – Mr Cox, her usual medical attendant, summoning London physicians in consultation – her constitution proved too enfeebled to resist the attack. The end came shortly before midnight on Thursday 22nd February – eleven days before her 77th birthday'.

Fortunately for us, she had always been concerned with posterity. Following John's death she had determinedly begun 'to set her house in order, arranging all her collections, weeding out things not really important, and putting together papers and facts about family history and the history of the Castle, which would make it more interesting and complete to those who were to follow her. Her unfinished catalogue of the contents of every room is most delightful reading and required infinite research and pains', said Bessie Calrow. The flint instruments and clay pipes, which she had paid the local ploughboys sixpence a time to find, were mounted and displayed in hanging cases.

Members of the Brocklehurst family, particularly her nephew Johnny, had continued to send her curious and interesting articles from their travels, but she had been very downcast when Marianne would not accept her offer of £1,000 to give her Egyptian collection to Sudeley Castle. Marianne was determined to find a home for it in Macclesfield, and in 1897 she and Peter founded the West Park Museum, with Peter, who had just handed over the Brocklehurst Bank to the Manchester and Liverpool District Banking Company, providing a full endowment for the museum.

Unfortunately neither Marianne nor Peter were able to be present at the opening ceremony for their museum in 1898 – and their cousin Francis Dicken Brocklehurst represented the family on this occasion. Marianne had slipped and fallen, while carrying some books upstairs at her London home, breaking her collarbone, and Peter was on his Scottish moor and not prepared to interrupt his shooting season. Marianne never recovered from her accident and died in October 1898 – a loss which Emma felt deeply.

Despite her own near blindness – she had a cataract operation on her other eye in the year before her death – she had continued to take a lively part in the affairs of Winchcombe. Lord Sudeley finally managed to persuade her to accept the advowson of Winchcombe, which also meant her increasing the living by £100 per annum. He himself was near bankruptcy, and Emma later reported the break up of his affairs – 'Toddington gone for their lifetime, the Welsh property and the London house to be sold.' Lady Sudeley came to make her farewells and kissed her for the first and last time.

She also continued to tease the local Radicals by hoisting the blue flag at the Castle when the Conservatives won a majority on the Parish Council, of which she had become Chairman. 'A fight in Winchcombe nearly followed, as they vowed they would take it down and there was the cry of 'Down with the Castle' – surely we are passing through a great revolution. Thank God at present it is bloodless', she commented.

Such upheavals seem far removed from the gentle picture Bessie Calrow paints of Emma's last days, in her obituary in the Cheltenham Ladies College Magazine of Spring 1900. 'The beautiful old lady, with the gracious presence, who ever was the loveliest part of that old Castle, standing like a Sir Joshua, or a Gainsborough, in the setting of the old doorway, to speed the parting guest. Or they may see her rising from the table, where the strangers had been hospitably entertained, opening the casement, and scattering the remains of the bread, or grain, which always stood in readiness for the lovely white pigeons, who were all waiting anxiously under the eaves of the roof, ready to circle round and alight, a snowy, fluttering crowd, the minute they heard the click of the window fastener. And when they had eaten every crumb and went to drink from their own special stone saucers on the edge of the quadrangle she would turn and say with a smile, 'And are they not like Pliny's doves?''.

THE LADY OF SUDELEY

The Cheltenham Ladies College Principal, Dorothea Beale, writing in the same publication, recalls Emma's delight in being able to share Sudeley – 'The grounds she did not consider her own – every rural entertainment was held there, and so far from this Englishwoman's home being, in the proverbial sense, her castle, it was seldom that one did not meet some visitors who had asked permission to walk through the rooms. I think of the pleasant Shakespeare readings that she arranged, of the lectures and entertainments she provided, of the gift slipped quietly into the carriage for a poor governess I had brought, of the note containing a cheque, passed without a word into the hands of a missionary.

Let me give you a few instances of her acts of thoughtful kindness. One Christmas that I passed at Sudeley I found she had spent nearly the whole of one night in arranging gifts for all the cottagers, thinking how many children there were, and what each would specially like'.

'We were out driving together, when a labouring man slipped off a cart. He was at once lifted into her carriage and taken to the Cottage Hospital, and then we drove on to his wife, lest she should first hear of the accident from others and be alarmed'.

There were also more gifts for Winchcombe. To mark the Diamond Jubilee of Queen Victoria in 1897 Emma gave to the parish church 'a deep toned bell on which the hours would be struck sufficiently loud to be heard at the Castle' and a preaching cross, and later she presented a new stone screen and stone statues. More unusually for the Victorian era she spent £400 on an open-air public swimming bath for the town, although there was to be 'no mixed bathing'.

Among her last papers is a letter she wrote to Harry and Marion describing the earthquake at Sudeley in December 1896:

'All safe – I felt the quake very distinctly, thought at first it was Tip shaking himself, then that Colonel Hinde who was in the next room had a fit of some sort – then that wagons were being driven under my window – then that it was a positive earthquake. I comforted myself by information given me a long time ago by some professor (who came to install lightning conductors in the Castle) that we were comparatively safe from earthquakes here with three solid miles of stone under us'.

It had been one of her great disappointments that Harry and Marion had not been able to spend more time with her at Sudeley. Even with his own farming responsibilities at Roel Harry was seldom on hand, while Emma complained that Marion would not often let the children visit her. Jack and Geoffrey were now at Eton and with their sister Marjorie they were dutifully allowed to come to help Emma celebrate the inauguration of the North Tower and again for the inauguration of the new drive and bridges. The death of Marion's father in 1892 had left her heir to Middlethorpe Hall, the family home in Yorkshire and also given Harry the chance to become owner of his small thoroughbred stud, all of which kept him away from Gloucestershire for long periods.

Johnny meanwhile was holed up defending Ladysmith during its siege in the Boer War, where he was in command of the Cavalry Brigade. He had also recently been appointed equerry to Queen Victoria and one of Emma's last pleasures was to hear that the Queen herself had sent a message to Ladysmith to enquire how General Brocklehurst was.

Among Emma's legacies was an unusual one to Martin Coucher de Meric. He was descended from the Couchers – her husband's mother's family – and she had come across him when his parents returned to Gloucestershire to restore the 300-year-old family home at Woodmanton.

Emma appeared to feel guilty about Sudeley passing to the Brocklehursts. In 1888 she gave the de Meric's a copy of the *Wysham/Coucher Pedigree Book*, with an added hand-written note beneath John's name saying 'Owner of Sudeley Castle, Winchcombe which he left to his wife's nephew – expected always to go to Mr C.C. de Meric his own blood descendant'. Young Martin was to receive his legacy on condition that he changed his name from de Meric to Coucher Dent, so that he ended up being called Martin John Coucher Dent Coucher.

Other gifts were £500 for the Chandos Almshouses in Winchcombe and £5 each to the inmates of the Dents Almshouses, £1 each to the teachers at Dents School and to each child there 2s 6d and a black frock. She also left £700 to the church at Hurdsfield for the benefit of the Church National Day School and the Sunday School there.

But her most lasting legacy lives on in Winchcombe and Sudeley. Dr. John Taylor in a moving sermon he preached the Sunday after her death said: 'To any stranger visiting Winchcombe it would be hardly too much to say 'If you would see her monument look around'. The architecture of the town bears the impress of her hand. The preservation of its picturesqueness was largely owing to her loving care'.

He recalled her own 'singular gifts – a clear mind, a retentive memory, a ready wit and a strong will – No-one could come into contact with her without receiving the impression of a vigorous personality. A French archaeologist who happened to meet her in the church turned to me after she had gone and exclaimed enthusiastically, 'But she is a queen''.

'How inquisitive of truth she was, unable to rest content unless she saw it with her own eyes. Christ now may be trusted to deal with her eager, inquiring mind.'

'Blessed, indeed, she was in many ways, with strength of body and mind, with good health, with large means, her lot cast in a pleasant pasture. But not every blessing was hers – she was childless, husbandless and for many years solitary. A really good woman; one who will be very considerably missed; one whose steadfast pursuit of the path of duty it might be well for us all to imitate. She rests from her labours'.

Future generations have also paid their tributes. Eleanor Adlard in her *Winchcombe Cavalcade* wrote: 'Mrs Emma Dent was not only a distinguished writer and a mine of local history but a great and beautiful lady – she was a sort of guardian angel to the district – keenly interested in its present as well as its past and to her the Castle owes its wonderful collection of local antiquities. And John Whittle, who was hall boy at the Castle in the 1930s and whose family came from Gretton, said that her building of the church and school there had transformed the village, where she was considered as 'saintly' – 'if you were on your uppers she would help you'.

But if Emma's presence is still felt in Winchcombe and the surrounding district, it is even more obvious at Sudeley, as Elizabeth Ashcombe dicovered when, having successfully turned her much-loved family home into a commercial enterprise, she found herself strangely drawn to the Long Room over the stables. Often used by Emma for parties, dances and theatricals – she had a stage built at one end – it was now piled high with boxes and trunks which had stood there untouched for nearly a century. As she began to unpack them; all Emma's stored treasures, diaries and memories were discovered and have now been collected and displayed to form a permanent exhibition of her life and times.

These were her bones, but I like to think that her spirit lives on in the great avenue of beech trees which she planted on the main drive to the Castle, so that they would 'grow up and cast their pretty shadows and spread their arms to catch the rays of the sun – and men and women would walk by them and children play under them, even when there was no-one left to remember the old lady who lovingly planted them'.